Coast Tales

TRUE HISTORIC STORIES FROM GEORGIA'S GOLDEN ISLES

BY LARRY HOBBS | The Brunswick News

THE BRUNSWICK
NEWS
THEBRUNSWICKNEWS.COM

Introduction

"The past is never dead. It's not even past."
William Falkner, Requiem for a Nun.

To be certain, the past is very much alive around these parts. For anyone paying even the slightest bit of attention, history's hold on the present is unavoidable. We are a part of it. Our journey is simply a continuation of their story.

In these ensuing passages gleaned from roughly a year's worth of my weekly History columns in The Brunswick News, our yesteryears intersect often with contemporary times. In some cases, such as Hofwyl-Broadfield Plantation or nearby Needwood Baptist Church in northern Glynn County, the storylines run uninterrupted through multiple generations, from then until now.

Landmarks, monuments or actual structures serve as reference points for those who came before us in still other accounts, be it the Horton House on Jekyll Island, Fort Frederica on St. Simons Island, or the remnants of the six slipways that launched newly-constructed World War II Liberty Ships into the Brunswick River.

Still other stories contained herein live on in legacy, from the African-inspired music of the Gullah Geechee culture's Ring Shouters to ye Olde English street names and public squares in historic Brunswick.

And yes, there might just be a ghost story or two inside: hints that the specter of a slain lightkeeper haunts our island lighthouse, or the peace offering erected to the disturbed remains of Brunswick's dearly-departed pioneers in Hanover Square.

Our Golden Isles forebears have much to tell us about ourselves in the many Coast Tales I have had the pleasure of chronicling thus

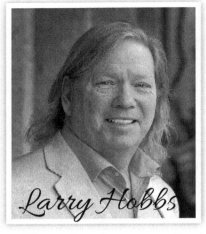

Larry Hobbs

far. It started with my documenting two years ago of respected local historian Buddy Sullivan's annual six-week lecture series for the Coastal Georgia Historical Society, which resulted in my little book with the big title: A Historical Crash Course on Coastal Georgia and the Golden Isles. It has sold generously at local venues and has been well received by the public, for which I am most grateful.

Through chance and circumstance, I presently have the privilege and opportunity to delve deeper into our past with the aforementioned weekly History column in The News. The responsibility has awakened a lifelong love of history within me, while instilling a new and unexpected sense of purpose in my mission as a newspaperman.

History is often a moving target, a valuable lesson I've learned while trying to narrow down a topic that only broadens with research as that weekly deadline looms ever closer. It sounds cliché, but I have a new appreciation for that notion about a thing being a labor of love.

But the response from readers has made the time and effort more than worthwhile. Quite a number of you have suggested it would be helpful to compile these historic pieces into a compendium of sorts. A book, perhaps?

That brings us to this, Coast Tales. Catchy title, huh? Coast? Ghost? For the record, I don't much believe in ghosts. Besides, as long as we keep their stories fresh and relevant, they live on with us. By the way, this book would not have been possible without the assistance and encouragement of my awesome boss. I am most grateful to Buff Leavy, Publisher of The Brunswick News.

So, turn the page and see where we have been — and how we got here.

History dead? It's not even past, y'all.

P.S. This book is dedicated to my sweetheart, Wylie.

Contents

PART 1: ST. SIMONS ISLAND

08 Island's original natives thrived on the bounty of land and water

11 Battle of Bloody Marsh was more bluff than blood, but a crucial British victory

14 History's mysteries come to life for Ft. Frederica archaeologist

18 Old Ironsides' tough reputation rooted in St. Simons Island Oak

21 Famous Revolutionary War date also has significance for local Naval Action victory

24 History's odd couple split over slavery during visit to Antebellum plantations

27 Butler family plantations sparked generations of intrigue on St. Simons Island

30 Methodist founder Wesley's short stay on St. Simons marked by dejection

33 Christ Church endures as spiritual center of St. Simons Island through four centuries

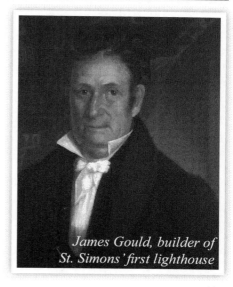

James Gould, builder of St. Simons' first lighthouse

36 Beloved invader's island time was spent in selfless, bitter sweet call to service of others

39 Construction of island's first lighthouse shines in capable hands of beloved author

42 St. Simons lighthouse II: From gunshots to ghosts stories, it just keeps on shining

46 Igbo Landing a defiant act for freedom

49 A new twist in Neptune Small's story only strengthens legacy

53 Island dispatches from the 19th century

56 For Island's African American community, there are no strangers at Union Memorial

59 Prominent black newspaper publisher's descendants foster his legacy locally

62 Millie Wilcox preserves Island's history through mother's artwork, Southern charm

66 Woman devoted life to singing Geechee's praises, preserving unique musical heritage

69 Redfern: An almost historic name, this pilot's final flight was launched from Sea Island

72 Hazel's Cafe endures today as a throwback to Island's past

PART 2: BRUNSWICK

Wright Square

76 Brunswick's Olde English roots remain

79 Carr's place in early Brunswick history changes, but endures

83 Wright Square: Digging up bones reveals city's tough start

86 Dart family tree branches out in Brunswick

89 Sidney Lanier: Man who famously put the marshes to rhyme was more than a poet

92 Brunswick-Altamaha Canal misses the boat

95 Opulent Oglethorpe Hotel once stood as crowning Jewel of downtown Brunswick

98 Call to Worship has deep roots in downtown Brunswick

101 Temple's tale that of the American dream

105 Port of Brunswick served valuable role in the cause of liberty during World War II

108 Nothing nostalgic about 1915's mass shooting in Brunswick

111 Portuguese fishermen helped launch Georgia's shrimp industry

115 Hollywood comes calling in Golden Isles

118 Local civil rights struggle was Quiet Conflict

121 Old Sidney Lanier Bridge marked by tragedy, endurance

PART 3: GOLDEN ISLES

124 Compared to the Spanish explorers, Oglethorpe was a historical newcomer

127 Horton House still stands as a link to Jekyll's early settlement

130 Fort King George's "invalid regiment" laid groundwork for future city of Darien

133 Hofwyl-Broadfield: Rice plantation endures as living history dating to Antebellum era

136 Hofwyl-Broadfield's little kepi has big story

139 Jekyll Island: From elite retreat to public treasure

142 Tom Floyd's journey: Tale of the Wanderer

145 State Holiday still rebel memorial for some

148 From slave to soldier to farmer, freedom rings in Major Magwood's inspired journey

151 Family tree grew strong within rural Needwood community

155 Modest vessel Kit Jones left big wake in history of Sapelo Island, Coastal Georgia

158 Deaconess Alexander: Footprints of a saint

161 Cutting edge 1900s technology, immigrants spurred local shrimping industry

Island's original natives thrived on the bounty of land & water

On quiet Sunday mornings, when light breezes gently stir the thick salt air through this moss-cloaked oak grove, you can almost feel their presence among us still.

St. Simons Park sits in tranquil indifference to the bustle of the Pier Village shopping district below it, or the condominium complexes that line Mallery Street one after another above it. Long before the British colonists arrived here, or the Spanish missionaries before them, Coastal Georgia was prime real estate for folks who had for ages called this "New World" home.

St. Simons Park was the setting for a thriving village of about 200 people from the Mocama tribe. They tilled the land to reap a bounty of produce that remains recognizable to us today at our local farmer's market, from peas and cantaloupe to squash and corn. The land around them and the waters that surrounded it rewarded their labors with an abundance of fish and game.

"There was plenty of game and fish, crabs, shrimp and oysters," said Buddy Sullivan, a noted author and Coastal Georgia historian, "A lot of the things we go into Publix to buy today were grown first by Native Americans. You should never go hungry on the Georgia Coast."

Evidence of human habitation along the coast and within its barrier islands dates back some 6,000 years. The Mocama and the Guale were the primary tribes in the area. The fertile geographic characteristics that have attracted folks to our coast for eons are rooted in the last ice age, 25,000 years ago.

Archeologists have determined the Mocama tribe established a village here on St. Simons Island.

Freshwater rivers flowing to the coast meet saltwater in estuaries like those at the Altmaha, Satilla and Ogeechee rivers. A rich breeding ground for marine life exists in the sounds between Coastal Georgia's eight barrier islands, where calm salt marsh waters flow to the open Atlantic Ocean.

"Coastal Georgia has more salt marsh than any other state on the Eastern Seaboard," Sullivan said. "Georgia has more salt marsh than South Carolina, which has twice as much coastline as us."

These ideal conditions supported a bustling community of Guale up on the north end of St. Simons Island. Evidence of their time here can be found in a "shell ring" within the Cannon's Point preserve off of Lawrence Road. Guale villages centered around circular walled structures that were comprised of felled trees. The natives shored up these walls with oyster shells and other leftovers from their seafood diets, building up over the generations into a rich trove of archaeological documentation.

A much larger shell ring exists on neighboring Sapelo Island. Archaeologists have determined the village encampment was nearly 300 feet across and up to 25 feet high. Numerous other refuse middens and burial sites have since been discovered at the site, dating back perhaps more than 4,000 years.

While evidence of permanent settlement is scant on Jekyll Island, native hunting and fishing expeditions there are well documented.

First contact with Europeans on Georgia's coast may have come as early as 1564, with the short-lived Fort Caroline, a French Huguenot outpost. Earlier speculation placed this French settlement in Florida near St. Augustine, but some scholars are convinced that evidence of the fort waits to be uncovered on the Altamaha River.

Any French intentions on occupation along the Atlantic coast were quickly trampled underfoot by the land-hungry Spanish. Spanish missionaries began arriving on these shores in the 1570s. Their most notable settlements here were Santo Domingo near present day Fort King George in Darien, San Buenos Ventura on the South End of St. Simons and Santa Catalina on St. Catherine's Island.

The two cultures co-existed for some time, but mistreatment and forced indoctrination led to the first uprising in 1597, which left at least five priests slain along the Coastal settlements.

Sadly, we all know how it turned out for the natives from this point. But at one time, the Guale alone sustained a population of some 4,000 people along our coast. They were thought to be off-shoots of the larger Creek tribe, which was centered in the Carolinas. Trading between these Creeks and Georgia's newcomers would become crucial to the colonists' survival.

The link between both cultures was Mary Musgrove, born around 1700 to a Creek mother and an English trader. Musgrove spoke both languages fluently and understood the needs that each culture brought to negotiations. She would flourish as the interpreter for Gen. James Oglethorpe in his dealings with the Creek during the peaceful establishment of Savannah.

These shores and the people who settled them would never be the same. But take a stroll through St. Simons Park some quiet Sunday morning.

Listen to the gentle rustle of ghostly old oaks in soft salty breezes. The imprint they left behind is with us still.

Battle of Bloody Marsh was more bluff than blood, but a crucial British victory

Likely as not, "Bloody Marsh" was just a British expression condemning the oppressive South Georgia heat on the day of the battle that is linked in time with St. Simons Island.

The Battle of Bloody Marsh was a monumental conflagration to be sure, both locally famous and historically significant on a global scale. But most historians agree that in terms of blood shed this conflict hardly lives up to its name.

One thing is pretty certain, however. If you were a British soldier marching out in full woolen uniform from Fort Frederica to thwart the Spanish advance, it must have been "bloody sweltering" on July 7, 1742. Regardless, the real fighting on St. Simons Island went down earlier that day at a swampy hollow not far from the fort called Gully Hole Creek.

Together, however, these two Colonial Georgia showdowns resulted in a resounding victory for British sovereignty in the Americas. The battles ended all designs Spain held on expanding north of Florida in Colonial America. It was all part of a larger war waged between Spain and Britain, presumably over the loss of British sea merchant Robert Jenkins' ear to an irate Spanish captain's sword. The two nations would continue to clash at several compass points abroad, but the War of Jenkins Ear effectively ended in this region that day on St. Simons Island.

The island's present-day intrigues, from stressed sewer pipes to Pier Village parking, fairly pale in comparison. But reminders of that historic day nearly 275 years ago abound among us still. It begins at Fort Frederica National Monument, where the remains of the island's original British settlement are lovingly

Bloody Marsh Battle Site national monument.

maintained by park rangers and volunteers. We drive daily past relevant historic markers connected to the battles. There is one on Demere Road recognizing the old Military Road the Spanish used to march on Fort Frederica after landing on the island's south end. Another historic marker, on Frederica Road near Christ Church, confirms where the Battle of Gully Hole Creek unfolded.

And then there is Bloody Marsh Battle Site, a small national monument tucked into the bend on Old Demere Road. Most historians agree there is no way of telling if this is where they fought the actual battle. But it does offer perhaps the island's most tranquil view of the marsh. It also features a granite monument, which echoes British Gen. James Oglethorpe's fighting words that day. Oglethorpe assures posterity, "We are resolved not to suffer defeat. Rather we will die like Leonidas and his Spartans ..."

Perhaps a little over-the-top in hindsight. But, of course, Oglethorpe could not have known that at the time. By the most scholarly of estimates, however, just seven of the roughly 2,000 Spanish troops who landed on St. Simons Island gave their last full measure in the scrap on Bloody Marsh.

But by then Oglethorpe had already demoralized the Spanish with a punishing blow at Gully Hole Creek, not far from the walls of Fort Frederica. It was there that Oglethorpe, some Scottish Highlander guerrillas and native volunteers met the initial Spanish advance of about 250 soldiers with a savage ambush. Oglethorpe's hastily mustered band of warriors killed 12 and captured 10 of the enemy, prompting the Spanish to beat a hasty retreat back down that military road that got them there.

What happened later that day at the so-called "Bloody Marsh" was actually a heroic bluff on the part of Oglethorpe and his undermanned force, many historians agree. At its peak, Fort Frederica and its adjacent township never held more than 1,000 troops and colonists.

But after the final salvos were fired at Bloody Marsh that day, Spanish leader Manual de Montiano convinced himself that his numerically superior forces were vastly outnumbered. A Spanish prisoner was intentionally released from Fort Frederica, returning to his commanders with intimidating and overrated accounts of British manpower.

Scouting ships arriving at the fort from Charleston, S.C., several days later unintentionally sealed the ruse for Montiano. His troops sailed back to St. Augustine about a week later, never to campaign north of there again.

The lone British death that day resulted from heat stroke at Gully Hole Creek. It must have been bloody hot that day.

History's mysteries come to life for Ft. Frederica archaeologist

Michael Seibert stepped into a knee-deeppit on the grounds of Fort Frederica National Monument one day in May as if he were dropping in on old neighbors.

Make that really old neighbors. The likes of Maj. William Horton and Richard Oldner have not been seen around these parts for nearly 300 years. Nonetheless, Seibert spoke of the two 18th century settlers with a familiarity and immediacy that suggested they were right here among us on this beautiful June day in 2018.

With Seibert serving as interpreter, I was granted an introduction of sorts. The latest neighborhood gossip concerning these two gentlemen unfolded on the close-shaved walls of this rectangular pit, written in the language of archaeology. It was a head-scratcher for Seibert, the onsite archaeologist at Fort Frederica, a British settlement in Colonial Georgia beginning in 1736.

The fort at one time was home to a military outpost and township, consisting of some 1,000 soldiers and colonists in its heyday. Archaeological digs at the site go back to the 1940s, providing us with a solid understanding of the township's layout and the people who occupied it.

Which brought us back to the mystery Seibert puzzled over last week while standing in that hole in the ground. The thing was, no one has ever said anything about a house on this particular plot, he said.

Its first owner was Oldner, a planter and a boatsman.

"In '38, he was asked by (Gen. James) Oglethorpe to teach soldiers the art of cultivation," Seibert said, referring to 1738. "He got paid for it. But after '39, Oldner disappears from the records."

Archaeologist Michael Seibert inspects a recent dig at Fort Frederica.

Standing in the pit with the sun shining down from cloudless skies, Seibert took a glance at the smooth side of the pit's wall. It was layered in earthen shades of pale sand, red clay and beige compost. Seibert picked up the story where he left off.

"Then along comes Horton," he said.

Horton, of course, was Gen. Oglethorpe's second in command at Fort Frederica. He had settled by then on a Jekyll Island plantation, now a popular attraction known as Horton House Historic Site. His remaining ties to St. Simons Island, however, included the plot in question. He fenced it in and planted a garden. But on visits to St. Simons Island, Horton stayed at the home of his friend Frances Moore.

"He encloses the whole lot and plants a garden," Seibert said, as if I knew this already. "But at no point in time is there a mention of a house being here, or any other substantial structure."

So, who said anything about a house being there in the first place? this visiting novice wondered. Well, hello!?!? It is all right there, Seibert said, written in red clay about halfway down the excavated wall.

Red clay does not occur naturally within the sandy soil of Coastal Georgia's barrier islands, Seibert reminds me, his enthusiasm for archaeological sleuthing growing contagious. However, red clay was a known building material for floors and foundations. The dig in this particular hole also unearthed bits of brick tabby, the mix of oyster shells, lime and sand so long a staple of coastal home construction, Seibert said.

"The clay is odd, we don't have clay here," Seibert said. "Wherever that came from, it had to be imported. So this looks like the floor of a structure. There should be no house here, and yet here we are."

The neck of a colonial-era glass wine bottle poked neatly out of the wall on the other side of this pit. Protruding from the smoothly-carved wall like some kind of 3D abstract art piece, the bottle will remain for now. Plenty of bottles were excavated for display during previous archaeological digs, including the last significant dig in the late 1970s. It was not worth compromising the integrity of this pit's parameters to take out one more bottle, he said.

"You don't want to pull things out of the side of the wall and risk messing up the profile," he explained. "It can cause issues. We just

16

cleaned it off and took some pictures and we're just going to leave that as it is."

Filter cloth will be spread over the pit's outline and a few contemporary coins will be tossed inside before the hole is refilled with dirt. This way, anyone poking around here in the future will know to pick up where Seibert and his crew left off.

This pit was just one of about a dozen excavated at various locations on the grounds of Fort Frederica during this recent dig, which began May 31 of 2018 and wrapped up Thursday. For those like Seibert who are fluent in the language of archaeology, each hole in the ground had a story to tell.

When I arrived on this day, Seibert was standing in yet another pit nearby, excavation trowel in hand. Already, a top layer of this pit's wall revealed the outline of a residential dirt road from the early 20th century. Below that were dark remnants of a fence post, most likely going back to the Taylor or Stevens families' time here during the 19th Century, Seibert said.

But Seibert was digging deeper still, shaving off a thin layer from the flat bottom of the pit. An object caught his eye and he bent down to pick it up. Smiling, he handed it up to me with dirty fingers.

"It's a piece of a pipe stem," he said. "You would be the second person to touch that in 200 years. It's Colonial."

Holding it in my hand, I felt a sudden immediacy and familiarity with those early European settlers from so long ago. It is Seibert who has it right after all. History is indeed alive at Fort Frederica National Monument.

Old Ironsides' tough reputation rooted in St. Simons Island Oak

From time immemorial, the powerful British Navy remained the rarely disputed ruler of the world's open seas.

Occasional challengers to this claim included France and Spain, but those upstart young Americans had no navy to speak of as the 19th century dawned. Then, on the afternoon of Aug. 19 in the year 1812, the new kid on the high seas flexed his muscles.

A crewman aboard the USS Constitution spied the sails of the British navy frigate Guerriere on the distant horizon. And American Capt. Isaac Hull closed in to challenge that royal reputation. The Guerriere and the Constitution squared off with scarcely 50 yards between the two warships and commenced to unload a point-blank cannonade upon each other with everything they had.

When the smoke cleared, there was nothing left of the Guerriere worth salvaging. The 44-gun Constitution, however, stood tall in the water, brandishing a new nickname that would echo through the annals of American history up to this very day.

"At this time the Constitution had received but little damage," Hull noted dryly in his official report of this naval engagement some 750 miles off the New England coast during the War of 1812.

In the heat of that battle, however, one U.S. sailor put it more bluntly: "Huzza! Her sides are made of iron!" And thus, the legend of "Old Ironsides" was born.

The ship's tough-as-iron reputation is rooted on St. Simons Island — literally. Old Ironside's framework and a layer of its hull were constructed of live oak felled at Gascoigne Bluff on St. Simons Island. The hull also was layered with white oak obtained elsewhere, but it was the dense composition of our local oaks that made the ship such a formidable foe, the experts say.

"This heavy timber has a density of 75 pounds per cubic foot, making it heavier than water, heavier than most other common timbers," according to an article on the American Society of Civil Engineers' website. "The huge internal braces of the ship were cut in solid pieces from individual trees, as opposed to being compositely joined on site. The result was a hard body that appeared to deflect cannon balls like iron."

The live oaks on St. Simons Island had grown without interference for ages, leaving the stately old trees with a unique shape and size that caught the eye of Boston shipbuilder Joshua Humpreys. President George Washington had tasked Humpreys in the early 1790s with building a naval fleet that could protect American interests on the high seas.

Constitution was the third of six ships that were eventually built under the congressional Naval Act of 1794. Knowing the young nation would always be outnumbered at sea, Humphreys set out to build warships that were bigger, faster and stronger.

He decided that the live oaks on St. Simons Island would be an integral part of that new navy's strength. The effort launched a timber boom at Gascoigne Bluff, where a mill was constructed beside the deep-water port on the Frederica River. Dozens of experienced ax men and carpenters were recruited from Connecticut to run the operation, which also used local white laborers and enslaved blacks from island plantations.

Recent Massachusetts transplant James Gould, the man who would eventually build St. Simons Island's first lighthouse, assisted the enterprise in locating and acquiring the most favorable timber. The local live oak's gargantuan, sharply curved limbs were particularly attractive to Humphreys and shipwright John T. Morgan.

As noted by the engineers in the passage above, these limbs could be cut to fit into the hull's framework in single pieces. Lightweight molds of the ship's pieces were crafted up north of durable paper or canvass, then hauled into the island's oak groves to determine which limbs measured up to the specifications.

The cut and milled timber was shipped to Boston, where the construction of the new navy occurred. The first three ships produced were the United States, the Constellation and the Constitution, which was christened in 1797.

The Constitution served in a minor maritime scuffle with France in the late 1790s and again in our war with Barbary Coast pirates in the early 1800s. But nothing in its resume gave the powerful British any inkling of what awaited them from America's still-wet-behind-the-ears navy.

What the HMS Guerrier faced that day was a frigate that was reinforced with sturdy St. Simons Island live oak to be larger and more heavily armed than its foes. Long in the keel (304 feet) and narrow of beam (43 1/2 feet), the design of the Constitution and its sister ships "gave the hull a greater strength than a more lightly-built frigate."

The Guerrier's crew learned this all too well. "Hull had surprised the British with his heavier broadsides and his ship's sailing ability," according to one account. "Adding to their astonishment, many of the British shots had rebounded harmlessly off Constitution's hull."

Old Ironsides would destroy the HMS Java in its next battle later that year. It would go on to defeat the British ships Pictou, Cyane and Levant before war's end. Constitution remained on active duty up until 1881 and became a museum ship in 1907.

It remains the oldest commissioned ship in the U.S. Navy. Old Ironsides operates under the direction of a U.S. Navy crew and officers, serving as a National Historic Site docked in Boston Harbor.

Famous Revolutionary War date also has significance for local Naval Action victory

From the onset of the Revolutionary War, the Brits were always whining about how the Americans did not fight fair.

The bellyaching began on Day One, April 19, 1775, at the Battle of Lexington and Concord. That is when colonial minutemen dressed in homespun garb hid behind trees and unloaded a withering fusillade upon the proper British ranks in their bright red coats, driving the world's most powerful army back to Boston with its tail between its legs.

And then there was that time a contingent of the British Navy found itself up a creek without a paddle, outgunned and outfoxed by a hardy bunch of patriots in rowboats.

The former began with the "shot heard 'round the world" up in Massachusetts and is certainly familiar to all who have read this deep into a column devoted to history. The latter encounter may not be so recognizable, but it unfolded right here on the shores of the Golden Isles, culminating with the Georgia State Navy capturing three amply-armed British sailing ships.

The Frederica Naval Action occurred in 1778 on the marsh side of St. Simons Island. It too took place on April 19. Lest we forget either historic event, the local Sons and Daughters of the American Revolution hold a Patriots Day ceremony on the Saturday closest to April 19 in the Pier Village area of St. Simons Island. Replete with historical interpreters dressed in ragtag militia outfits and Continental Army blue uniforms, our local Patriots Day observance honors both the valiant stand at Lexington and Concord as well as the local blow for freedom on the same date three years later.

Those dedicated DAR and SAR members have hosted Patriots

Day for the past 14 years. It is a unique event for these parts, although Patriots Day has long been recognized as a state holiday in Massachusetts and Maine.

The cannon fire and musketry salutes on the green at Neptune Park are a perennial favorite of kids young and old during our ceremony. Gunpowder smoke and booming echoes float each year out toward the mouth of St. Simons Sound, from which the HMS Galatea retreated 240 years ago as the lone British ship to escape the Frederica Naval Action.

The British ships Hinchinbrook, Rebecca and Hatter were by then stuck in "Racoon Gut" on the Frederica River, abandoned by their crews under a barrage from those Georgia rowboats. Ok, rowboat is an understatement. But I could hardly resist the image.

These vessels were actually long galleys, made specifically for swift action under oar power in Coastal Georgia's fickle inland waters. The state's navy had four of these 70-foot galleys built in 1777, underwritten for Georgia shore protection by the Continental Congress.

The ships were pointed at bow and stern, 13 feet across at the beam and flat bottomed to affect a shallow draft. Two triangular sails could be raised in light winds, but mostly the galleys Lee, Washington, Bulloch and Congress were powered by patriot muscle pulling 22-foot-long oars along port and starboard. Each packed a heavy cannon on the bow, with smaller half-pound cannon and swivel guns along each side.

The British contingent in north Florida would not let the colonial bluster of this nearby naval presence go unanswered. Led by the Galatea, the brigantine Hinchinbrook, the sloop Rebecca and the brigantine Hatter set out to destroy Georgia's little fleet.

All four British ships were loaded for mayhem, heavily armed with 14- to 9- pound cannon and plenty of sailors and marines to man them.

But word of British intentions to destroy Georgia's new navy soon reached Col. Samuel Elbert, a Savannah merchant who rose to command both Georgia's Continental Army and Navy. Rather than chart a course for safe harbor, Elbert went on the attack.

After weeks of fruitless searching by the Brits, the Georgians found them. By the evening of April 18, HMS Galatea was an-chored in the St. Simons Sound, with Hinchinbrook, Rebecca and Hatter stationed farther north on the Frederica River.

At daybreak the next morning, the Georgia galleys Washing-ton, Lee and Bulloch went on the offensive, coming bow-first at the British sailing ships. In such tight waters, the British already were outmaneuvered. Lined up bow-to-stern of the oncoming galleys, the firepower on either side of the three British ships was rendered useless.

The marsh tides and breezes also would conspire on behalf of the patriots. There was no wind for the British sails and the inland tide was at its ebb, or low stage. The galleys anchored about a half mile away and opened up with a cannonade.

Seeking refuge, the Hinchinbrook inadvertently ran around in what the British called Raccoon Gut, quite possibly near what we know today as Dunbar Creek. Rebecca and Hatter followed suit. Actually, the British did have a paddle as it turns out. Under heavy fire, the crews loaded into the ships' rowboats and beat a hasty retreat to the Galatea on the St. Simons Sound.

The Georgia State Navy seized all three sailing ships. While not nearly so stirring as that patriotic stand for Independence three years earlier at Concord and Lexington, it was a proud day for Georgia's freedom fighters.

"I have the happiness to inform you, that about 10 o'clock this forenoon, the Brigantine Hitchenbrooke, the Sloop Rebecca and (the Hatter), all struck the British Tyrant's colours, and surren-dered to the American arms," Col. Elbert wrote to his superiors.

History's odd couple split over slavery during visit to Antebellum plantations

Nearly 200 years after the fact, you still have to wonder just what the heck Fanny Kemble and Pierce Mease Butler were thinking — running off and getting married like that, a pair who could not have possibly been more incompatible.

Butler was a wealthy Philadelphian, poised in 1834 to inherit a family empire borne on the backs of mass human bondage at rice and cotton plantations along the Atlamaha River and on St. Simons Island.

And Frances Anne "Fanny" Kemble? Fanny was an adored 19th Century celebrity from London, a talented Shakespearean actress who was much in demand on American stages. She also was a strong-willed and highly-intelligent woman, an ardent abolitionist who made no attempt to conceal her vehement condemnation of slavery.

So, how did that work out? Not too well, as you might expect.

But before finally imploding in acrimony and scandal 15 years later, the marriage produced two daughters — and a scathing memoir decrying the deprivations of slavery. Fanny also was a prolific and gifted writer, as well as a keen observer of the human condition and the South's "peculiar institution." Her only visit to the Butler plantation down here produced *Journal of a Residence on a Georgian Plantation in 1838-1839.*

Her first-hand observations of slave life that winter during her four-month stay at Butler's two plantations would drive an irreconcilable wedge between the two. Fanny would soon return to England and resume her acting career. A marital separation in 1845 preceded the inevitable divorce in 1849.

Fanny resisted publishing her memoirs — a series of letters

Fanny Kemble: actress, writer, abolitionist

to a friend up north — for more than two decades, fearing retribution from Butler, who retained custody of their two girls. Her Journal was released first in England in 1863, a rebuttal to possible English intervention on behalf of the South in the Civil War that then raged in America.

For American abolitionists, the book served to validate all their worst fears. Most could only imagine the human suffering wrought by slavery; Fanny witnessed it firsthand.

"It is the closest, most-detailed look at plantation slavery ever recorded by a white northern abolitionist," a PBS historian noted.

She turned her keen eye on more than just the sins of slavery. Fanny was both enamored and alarmed by the teeming flora, fauna and climate of Coastal Georgia.

But the sequence of events that put this refined actress in the wilds of Georgia necessarily requires a little more background.

Pierce Butler was the grandson of Major Pierce Butler, a Revolutionary War veteran who built his fortune on the two local plantations. He owned more than 600 slaves, who toiled to produce rice on Butler's Island in McIntosh County and sea island cotton on St. Simons Island. One of the wealthiest men in America, he owned homes also in Charleston, S.C., and in Philadelphia, Penn.

Pierce Butler lived in Philadelphia, making winter junkets to their Georgia plantations to get a feel for the family business he would one day inherit.

The scion of one of the largest slave-holding families in America became infatuated with Kemble when he saw her perform in Philadelphia in 1832. Pierce could be something of a charmer, it was said.

A shining star in a family of actors, Fanny returned his affections. The marriage afforded her the opportunity to leave the stage and pursue her true passion, writing. This arrangement produced the best-selling *Journal of Frances Anne Butler* in 1835.

But differences of opinion put their marriage on the skids almost from onset, particularly on the issue of slavery. In 1838, Butler finally relented to her requests to join him on a trip to Georgia.

Excerpts from her plantation journal are insightful and sobering. We all know today that slavery of any form is detestable. In the context of 1830s America, it was still a subject for debate in most circles.

Kemble argues the obvious with clarity and skewering logic. An example: The contradiction created by the belief that slaves were "inferior" with the need for laws against teaching them academically. She writes "to this I can only reply, that if they are incapable of profiting by instruction, I do not see the necessity for laws inflicting heavy penalties on those who offer it to them."

Rather, she writes, "these themes are forbidden to slaves ... because they ... would seize on them with avidity ... and the masters' power over them would be annihilated at once and forever."

She was more forgiving of coastal Georgia's untamed beauty. Fanny described wildflowers encountered on a boating trip along the Altamaha as "the most beautiful gardenias I have ever beheld ... with their thick-leaved, cream-white odoriferous blossoms."

Some moments are even light-hearted, such as her fishing trip on the river with a savvy enslaved man named Jack. As a writer who also has separated more than a few catfish from the hook that caught them, I could not possibly improve on this proper Englishwoman's description of the steps necessary to avoid getting stung by the spiny fins.

She describes in detail the need to push the top spiked fin down while pushing the two spiked side fins up "before you can get any purchase on the slimy beast." But, she concludes, this renders "the catching of catfish questionable sport."

On that, Miss Fanny, we disagree.

Butler family plantations sparked generations of intrigue on St. Simons Island

On the north end of St. Simons Island, Pierce Butler Drive intersects with both Fanny Kemble and Aaron Burr streets — much like the figures' lives crossed paths here on the Georgia Coast in the 19th Century. Well, sort of.

We talked in the previous history column about how celebrity actress and ardent abolitionist Fanny Kemble married Pierce Mease Butler, a Philadelphian who owned hundreds of slaves at plantations on St. Simons Island and on Butler Island in McIntosh County. But there are enough footnotes and anecdotes branching out from that story to fill an entire book.

For starters, Butler was the grandson of Major Pierce Butler, the man who established the family fortune growing rice at Butler Island and sea island cotton on Hampton Plantation on St. Simons' north end. The elder Butler was an associate of Aaron Burr, the one-time U.S. vice president who is best known for his adversarial role in the most famous duel in American history. Yes, that Aaron Burr.

Born in Ireland in 1744, Butler arrived in America as a Major in the British Army. He served in Boston and later Charleston, S.C., where he met and married Polly Middleton. With the outbreak of the America Revolution, Butler resigned his post in the British Army and sided with the winners, serving in the Continental Army until war's end in 1782.

For all the ignoble baggage that would accompany Burr in later years, he too served America's Continental Army with distinction during the Revolution. He was instrumental in a whole regiment's successful escape from Manhattan during the continentals' pivotal retreat from New York. Burr saw heated action

This smokestack from the plantation mill on Butler Island still stands today.

later in the Battle of Monmouth.

Burr was serving as Jefferson's Vice President in 1804 when a war of political words with Alexander Hamilton led to a showdown with pistols on July 11 at Weehawken, N.J. Burr walked away unscathed; however, his shot fatally wounded Hamilton.

Dueling was beginning to be frowned upon in polite society; in fact, it had been outlawed in both New York and New Jersey. So after his duel with Hamilton, Burr absconded south to St. Simons Island, staying originally at Butler's Hampton Plantation. He later spent time on John Couper's Cannon's Point Plantation. In his roughly month-long stay here, Burr survived an "alarming" hurricane which "shook and rocked" Couper's plantation home, according to a Sept. 12 letter to his daughter. Earlier, Burr expressed an indifference for the low country's aesthetic charms.

"The country, of course, presents no scenes for a painter," he wrote. He wiled the rest of that day away thusly: "frightened some crocodiles (alligators), shot some rice-birds and caught some trout."

Burr later returned to the northeast, where all charges eventually were dropped. Later, Burr's reputation suffered more damage still when he narrowly escaped charges of treason, eluding allegations that he conspired with foreign agents to establish a new nation on the American frontier.

Major Pierce Butler died in 1822. Pierce Mease Butler was one of two surviving grandsons who inherited the major's estate around 1836, with the death of his unmarried daughter Frances Butler. Pierce was born a Mease but changed his surname to Butler in keeping with his grandfather's stipulation for inheritance.

Pierce and Fanny Kemble fell in love while the Shakespearean actress was performing in his hometown of Philadelphia. Her one and only visit to the Georgia Coast resulted in the *Journal of a Residence on a Georgian Plantation, 1838-1839*. By the time the book was published as the Civil War raged in 1863, this unlikely marriage had long-since crumbled. They had two daughters: Sarah, who sided with her mom on the issue of slavery; and Frances, who shared her dad's pro-slavery sentiments.

Fanny went back to England, but returned to America on and off, supporting herself as a writer and Shakespearean orator.

Butler squandered his fortune on gambling and bad investments. To pay off his debts, he orchestrated the largest single slave auction in our history. Known as "The Weeping Time," the auction in Savannah on March 2-3 of 1859 "consisted of 436 men, women, children and infants, being half the (slave) stock remaining on the old Major Butler plantations ... " according to a northern abolitionist newspaper's report.

After the Civil War, Pierce Butler and daughter Frances would attempt to revive the Butler's Island rice operations, enlisting former slaves to work the land as sharecroppers. During that time, Frances wrote "Ten Years on a Georgia Plantation Since the War," intended as a rebuttal to her mother's harsh assessment of slavery. Pierce Butler was managing the farm at Butler's Island in 1867 when he died of malaria. Frances and her husband, John Wentworth Leigh, would move to England in 1877.

Fanny died in 1893 in London.

Daughter Sarah would go on to marry Owen Jones Wister, a doctor from Philadelphia. They had a son, Owen Wister, who made his mark on the literary world by writing *The Virginian*.

Methodist founder Wesley's short stay on St. Simons marked by dejection

When John Wesley set sail for the fledgling British Colony of Georgia in 1735, the future founder of the Methodist Church was a man of timid faith whose theology was more academic than spiritual.

He returned to England two years later as a wanted man, heartbroken, disillusioned and grateful to be alive. St. Simons Island was the backdrop for much of his troubles in the New World, where the Anglican minister found love, wound up in the wrong corner of a love triangle, endured death threats and even dodged an attempt to shear his long auburn locks. Additionally, his faith was shaken by life-threatening storms on both transatlantic crossings.

Such trials and tribulations may well have informed Wesley's spiritual transformation, helping mold the charismatic preacher whose stirring sermons of God's Grace would later ignite an evangelical wave among the unwashed masses back in England. But although many locals reverently honor Wesley's time here, the man who would lay the foundation for the Methodist Church and plant the seeds of the Pentecostal movement was all too happy to leave St. Simons Island in his wake.

"He had a miserable time here," said the Rev. Dave Hanson, a local retired Methodist minister and Wesley historian.

Wesley's life and his influence on the protestant movement are the subject of nearly 400 biographies. But you will be hard-pressed to find anyone more knowledgeable than Hanson about Wesley's short time on St. Simons Island. Hanson's popular lecture, "John Wesley on St. Simons Island," is presented free to the public at 2 p.m. each Thursday at the Arthur J. Moore Methodist Museum and Library at Epworth by the Sea.

Along with his brother Charles, Wesley came here as a minister to Gen. James Oglethorpe's debtor's Colony of Georgia. While the Anglican minister spent most of his 23 months in Georgia at the colony's home base of Savannah, he also made several visits to St. Simons Island, where Oglethorpe was busy building a settlement around Fort Frederica.

Wesley made five trips to the island, spending a total of about 100 days here. He was meticulous about keeping his journal, and Hanson has scoured every detail regarding his time on St. Simons Island.

"I have read everything I can find about his 100 days on the island," said Hanson, who was pastor of St. Simons United Methodist Church for seven years before retiring in 2003.

The son of a preacher, Wesley initially took the scholarly approach to his calling, immersing himself in 15 years of theological studies at Oxford's Church of Christ College. He met Oglethorpe through his association with The Holy Club, a devout group whose service work included ministering to those locked away in England's notorious debtors' prisons.

In October of 1735, the Wesley brothers found themselves sailing for Georgia aboard the Simmonds. They had a terrible time crossing the Atlantic. The last of three vicious storms nearly sunk the Simmonds. Many a passenger shrieked in terror for their very lives, but none wailed more loudly than Wesley.

His panic was in stark contrast to the calm demeanor of the German Moravians on board, who peacefully sang hymns through the tempest. When Wesley asked how they faced death with such tranquil acceptance, the Moravians responded with a ques-

This marker near Christ Church commemorates the Wesley brothers stay here.

tion of their own: "Mr. Wesley, do you know Christ as your Savior?"

The elusive answer began the soul-searching that would lead to Wesley's transformation.

But not yet. Wesley's sermons of the day were weary affairs mired in religious dogma, eliciting little more than yawns and tedium, Hanson said. Additionally, his heavy-handed enforcement of strict religious laws drew the ire of many a colonist. Upholding such laws as no gunfire on the Sabbath earned Wesley death threats. One irate wife even came at him with a pistol in one hand and shears in the other, bent on cropping Wesley's long-flowing locks.

Most troubling of all was his love life. One of Wesley's stated intentions in coming to Georgia was to avoid temptations of the flesh. But Wesley soon found himself smitten by Sophie Hopkey, a fetching young Savannah lass of just 18. But the 32-year-old Wesley was slow on the take. A smooth talker moved in and stole Sophie's heart.

The lovelorn Wesley lashed out by refusing communion to Sophie. In response, an arrest warrant was taken out on Wesley, charging him with public embarrassment by banning Sophie from communion.

Dejected and demoralized by his experiences in Georgia, Wesley sailed home for England in 1737.

However, a year later, on May 24, 1738, Wesley experienced his spiritual awakening at a gathering of the faithful Moravians in London. It marked the beginning of Wesley's evangelical crusade to preach salvation through Christ and grace. His message resonated with the lower rungs of society, folks heretofore overlooked due to the niceties of 18th century church etiquette. They gathered in the thousands at large outdoor venues to hear the rejuvenated preacher spread his message.

"He was the Billy Graham of his day," Hanson said.

Hanson also lectures on Wesley to church groups, civic organizations and others. For more information, contact him at jdavehanson@bellsouth.net.

Christ Church endures as spiritual center of St. Simons Island through four centuries

John Wesley's short, lovelorn stay in Georgia's young colony was largely forgettable from a personal standpoint, and surely better things awaited the Anglican pastor who would go on to establish the Methodist Church.

Nevertheless, Wesley left behind an indelible stamp here on St. Simons Island, one that endures still today. Several years before his stirring outdoor sermons would captivate believers by the thousands back in England, Wesley presided over modest open-air services beneath a moss-draped oak near Fort Frederica.

In one fashion or another, the site where that oak stood has served as a spiritual center on the island through four centuries — from 1736 up until this next Sunday, when the faithful will be called once again to worship at Christ Church, 6329 Frederica Road. Hanging in the church is a large cross crafted from the wood of that Wesley Oak, which fell to a 1956 hurricane. "Under which John and Charles Wesley preached at St. Simons Island, Georgia in the year 1736," it reads.

But that present church building is a mere 134 years old. It was built in the late 19th Century to replace the original Christ Church structure, which was destroyed by Yankee occupiers who bivouacked there in slovenly form during the Civil War years.

But this is hallowed island ground indeed, tied to virtually every prominent St. Simons family dating back to the Antebellum era and before. It also served as the plot-twist in a best-selling historical romance novel. The creators of both that romance and those deep family ties rest in its cemetery, as do many other notable folks from the island's long and storied history. Presi-

33

dents Calvin Coolidge, Jimmy Carter and George Bush have visited the church.

But we're getting ahead of ourselves. Let's back up.

Four years after founding the Colony for Georgia based in Savannah in 1732, Gen. James Oglethorpe laid the groundwork for Fort Frederica and its township. John Wesley and brother Charles Wesley arrived in Savannah in late 1735 to minister to the new colony.

Charles came first to St. Simons Island in March of 1736 as minister to the newly-arrived settlers, preaching the island's first sermon on March 17, 1736, beneath that Wesley Oak. John, then the minister of the new parish in Savannah, arrived several months later to find Charles in ill health. Charles returned to Savannah, and from there back to England for good. (No slacker despite his brother's accomplishments, Charles was a prodigious writer of enduring hymns, including the classic carol, "Hark! the Herald Angels Sing.")

John would return to St. Simons Island on at least two occasions in 1737, establishing a church in the community and preaching to the congregation during his stays there. The spiritual transformation that ignited his soul still awaited Wesley back in England, and his sermons under the Wesley Oak were probably stodgy yawners.

He returned to England later that year, nursing emotional wounds from a failed romance with a Savannah girl, as well as a congregation that smoldered with rebellion under his heavy-handed religious laws.

George Whitefield, a deacon for Frederica and Savannah who was appointed by the Bishop of London, preached also under the old oak during and after the Wesleys' time there. Whitefield and others from the Society for the Propagation of the Gospel preached the word there through 1766.

That early settlement faded, eventually giving way to a community of planter families and plantations. Revolution came, and a new nation established itself on these shores. As early as 1776, Episcopalian services were being held under that oak, or in the home of a local family when bad weather dictated.

Those planter families organized a parish in 1807, and a year later the charter for Christ Church was officially established by the state legislature. William Best was its first rector, followed by the Rev. Edmund Matthews in 1810.

The congregation then set about raising the money to build an actual church. But the young nation soon found itself at war with the best customer of the island's economic staple, cotton. An embargo on cotton to England followed a complete shutdown of trade between the two nations with the War of 1812, which did not end until 1815.

An actual church on the site of Christ Church did not rise until 1820. It was the only church on the island, serving people from 14 plantations. Edmunds remained its rector.

Years later, the well-regarded planter Thomas Spalding spoke on the occasion of the island's spiritual centennial in 1836. A year later, church leaders sold off all but 5 acres of church property to withstand the economic Panic of 1837.

With the outbreak of the Civil War, white islanders abandoned St. Simons Island to advancing Union troops in early 1862. Occupying troops quartered themselves in the church until war's end in 1865, making pigs of themselves by most accounts.

Returning islanders found the church's interior reduced to shambles, a gaping hole in its roof. Parishioners salvaged a few pews and a four-columned consecration table base. Then they returned to worshipping in the outdoors or in each other's homes.

So how did we get the beautiful Christ Church that stands today? It would require another Northern invader. A beloved one this time, or so the story goes.

Beloved invader's island time was spent in selfless, bittersweet call to service of others

In late 1879, a rich kid from up north came down to visit his daddy at the tycoon's lumber mill on St. Simons Island.

It proved to be an encounter of pivotal change for both the island and the young man. During a horseback jaunt only slightly longer than his name, Anson Greene Phelps Dodge Jr. came upon the tumbledown husk of post-Civil War Christ Church — and his life's destiny.1

At just 19 years young, Anson already had traveled extensively, visiting some of the most majestic old gothic churches of Europe along the way. But he was captivated by this rustic little wooden chapel tucked among the lazy oaks and thick salt air, recognizing immediately its spiritual significance to the islanders he would grow to love.

So began Anson's short, bittersweet life of service to others. He would rebuild Christ Church, become its ordained pastor, experience deep love and tragic loss, all before dying at the young age of 38. His story, along with that of the church he resurrected, is multidimensional and replete with nuance, ranging from the sublime to the downright strange.

No less famous is the tale's most capable narrator. You can read all about Anson and Christ Church in author Eugenia Price's historical romance novel, *The Beloved Invader*. Many of you no doubt already have read the best seller, the last in her trilogy of historically-accurate novels based on St. Simons Island. It is all there, including a kissing-cousin romance and Anson's decision to bury his dearly departed beneath the rebuilt church's altar.

Young Anson first arrived on St. Simons Island when the island was yet again reinventing itself, emerging from the ashes of the Civil War as a lumber mill community. With a timber boom bringing interior Georgia's tall pines down the Altamaha River to St.

Christ Church on St. Simons Island.

Simons Island, Anson Greene Phelps Dodge Sr. established a lumber mill on the island's Gascoigne Bluff, taking up residence in the former Hamilton plantation home.

The Dodge family was famous nationally, long known for both its wealth in mining and timber interests and its tradition of service to others. In fact, Anson's uncle was the Rev. David Stuart Dodge, a renowned clergyman involved worldwide in educational and philanthropic activities.

Anson's first love was the Rev. Dodge's daughter, Ellen Ada Phelps Dodge. This, of course, made the two lovebirds first cousins. Despite family protestations, their love would not be denied. After a failed elopement gained international press attention in 1878, the families eventually relented, and the cousins were married two years later.

The happy couple could have led a life of luxury, mixing in the highest circles of New York society. But Anson's course forever changed the day he saw Christ Church, which had been reduced to ruin by occupying Union forces during the war. Likewise, the island's prosperous prewar antebellum planter era had given way to folks living under frugal conditions that struck the young man of privilege as charmingly provincial.

Anson made up his mind: After their honeymoon, he and Ellen would settle on St. Simons Island. He would put his family fortune to good works by rebuilding Christ Church. Additionally,

Anson would attend New York's General Theological Seminary and become Christ Church's pastor.

But first, the newlyweds set out on a doozy of a globe-trotting honeymoon. In the third year of this whirlwind romantic sojourn, the two were in India when tragedy struck. Ellen succumbed to cholera, the result of eating unclean fruit.

Grief-stricken, Anson brought his bride's body home — home to St. Simons Island. Ellen was buried beneath the alter of the new Christ Church, rebuilt on the same site in 1884.

And the young widower soldiered on, completing divinity school and returning to minister to the growing flock on St. Simons Island. Anson also shepherded other churches across the island, including the congregation of freedmen at St. Ignatius. And Anson did find love again, this time to an island girl. Anna Gould was the granddaughter of James Gould, builder of the island's first lighthouse. As author Price tells the story, Anna and her father, Horace Bunch Gould, had been close acquaintances of Anson since his first visit to St. Simons Island.

His happiness was sealed in 1891 with the arrival of a son, Anson Greene Phelps Dodge III. Anson's joy again was short-lived. Little Anson was killed in 1894, thrown from a runaway horse buggy in front of the Dodge family home.

Finding strength through faith and service to others, Anson and Anna turned their energies toward opening the Anson Phelps Dodge Home for Boys at their home. Continually in and out of poor health during these latter years, Anson died on Aug. 20, 1898.

Selflessly, Anna had Anson's first love removed from her lone resting place beneath the church alter. Ellen was reinterred to rest beside Anson, beneath a shared tomb. Anson III rests beside them in the Dodge family plot at Christ Church cemetery, as does Anson's mother, Rebecca Dodge.

Anna was still operating the Dodge Home for Boys when she died in 1927 (the home closed in 1956). She too is buried in the family plot.

They rest within hearing distance of the hymns the congregation sings each Sunday at Christ Church, maintaining a spiritual link that began on these grounds some 280 years ago, beneath the Wesley Oak.

Construction of island's first lighthouse shines in capable hands of celebrated author

Even way back when he was a little kid growing up in land-locked western Massachusetts, James Gould wanted someday to build a lighthouse.

But this childhood fancy grows to dramatic proportions in the capable hands of author Eugenia Price, the beloved romance novelist famous for setting her characters on St. Simons Island.

"A dream," Gould tells his new bride in Price's 1971 bestseller, *Lighthouse*. "That's all they mean. A dream. I've nothing to show for it except these plans — for the one thing I've ever wanted to build."

Spoiler alert: James Gould goes on to build the first lighthouse on St. Simons Island, a 75-foot high structure completed late in 1810. But not without first going through heartache, triumph, tribulations galore, wilderness adventures in Spanish Florida, love, loss and laughter. It is all in included in *Lighthouse*, Price's fictional take on the real-life journey of the man who built it.

A friend loaned me Lighthouse not long ago, asserting that anyone writing about local history needs to read Price. I am an avid reader, but stomaching the syrupy stuff of romance novels has never sat quite well with me. But I heeded my friend's advice and tackled *Lighthouse.* Sure enough, not only is the story set locally, but its very pages must have been produced from our tall Georgia pines. Sap oozes from every page.

But Price (1916-1996), a West Virginian who fell in love with St. Simons Island and made it her home, was a diligent historian. She pored over family letters, government contracts, birth certificates and other documents long before Google searches came along, tracking down elusive records stretching from the

James Gould, builder of St. Simons'
first lighthouse.

Glynn County Public Library all the way to the National Archives in Washington, D.C. Adventure, romance and derring-do are fairly packed into her romantic page-turners, but Price's plots pretty much stick to the scripts history gave her.

And Price pays close attention to the details of those times. She places readers squarely in her books' setting with facts of life from the early 19th century, including flora and fauna, home lighting, horse carriage makes and models and inland navigation.

And in the interest of full disclosure, I am now 100 pages into the *Lighthouse*'s sequel (this was August 2017), *New Moon Rising*. No one goaded me into reading this one. And I won't sleep tonight without learning what has become of that headstrong young Horace Gould — the impetuous wayward son who ignores the sage advice of sister Mary and the pleadings of dear "Maum Larney," traipsing about in New Orleans institutions of questionable repute and on Mississippi gambling boats instead of returning home to the St. Clair Plantation where he belongs. Whew!

But it is perhaps fitting that Price would choose James Gould and his offspring to tell the story of turn-of-the-19th century St. Simons Island. Gould is perhaps typical of the heroic figures who for generations have constantly reinvented these shores and their place among them.

Gould was born in Granville, Mass., on the brink of the Revolutionary War in 1772. The son of Kate and Continental Army Capt. James Gould, the youngster grew up with a knack for building and a mindset for self-sufficiency.

James first arrived on St. Simons Island in the 1790s, part of the crew that felled massive oaks at Gascoigne Bluff for the construction of three warships for the young nation's emerging navy. Among those was the mighty 44-gun frigate U.S.S. Constitution, better known as "Old Ironsides."

The U.S. Congress had been seeking a builder for a lighthouse on St. Simons Island since as early as 1804. Gould answered that call in 1807. To save money, Gould suggested using the local mix of shells, sand and lime known as tabby in the construction of the thick-walled octagonal tower.

Great idea, concurred the folks in Washington, D.C. Gould's main source for tabby? That's right, he freely pilfered the ruins of Fort Frederica, the Colonial Georgia outpost built on the island in 1736 by British Gen. James Oglethorpe. Additionally, he used bricks from the fort to construct the 20-by-12-foot lamp-oil storage vault.

The lighthouse, the oil vault and the adjoining home for the lighthouse keeper were completed in late 1810, at a cost to the government of $13,775. It was 25 feet in diameter, topped by a 10-foot-high oil-burning lantern operated on a system of chains.

Gould must have been pleased with the finished product. He immediately applied for the open lighthouse keeper's job, a position he held for the next 27 years at a whopping salary of $400 annually. But he soon moved wife Janie and their growing family to St. Clair Plantation, 800 acres on which Gould built their home and grew long staple Sea Island cotton.

Gould died in 1852, 10 years before Confederate troops dynamited his Lighthouse to keep it out of Yankee hands during the Civil War. He is buried at Christ Church cemetery.

As for his youngest son, the defiant Horace Gould? Please, keep quiet if you know. I have not yet reached that part in Price's second novel of island intrigue.

St. Simons lighthouse II: From gunshots to ghosts stories, it just keeps on shining

Few folks pay attention to history when they are busy making it.

But from the distant perspective of an armchair historian, ironies abound.

James Gould recycled the abandoned ruins of St. Simons Island's first colonial settlement, Fort Frederica, to build the island's first lighthouse in 1810. Retreating Confederates blew up that 75-foot-high structure 51 years later to prevent its use by advancing Union troops during the Civil War. Thus, some of the ruins of 18th Century Fort Frederica became 19th Century rubble on the other end of the island.

Among the first returning islanders to view the Confederate demolition crew's handiwork was the war-weary Horace Gould, the oldest son of the now deceased James Gould. A reluctant rebel to the Union advances, Horace served as a captain in the Confederate Army and fought in the defense of Atlanta. Stoically, Horace would reclaim the family's Black Banks estate at war's end and live out the remainder of his life as a humble farmer and family man of strong faith.

And, as we all know, a new lighthouse rose even higher from in the wreckage of the post-Civil War era. That new 104-foot structure was designed by Orlando Poe, a West Point-trained architect who served as Union Gen. William T. Sherman's chief engineer during the sacking of Atlanta.

With so much to consider, it is easy to get distracted while peeking into the rabbit holes of our history. But the previous history column on the Golden Isles' first lighthouse necessarily led to this sequel about the one that followed.

And if James Gould's lifelong destiny to build that first one inspired Eugenia Price's romance novel *Lighthouse*, the early

Early photograph of the present St. Simons Lighthouse.

history of the succeeding lighthouse could have come from the mind of Edgar Alan Poe. It is a tale of triumph to be certain, but it is haunted with malaise, death, a cold-blooded killing and, of course, a good ghost story.

Horace had but little time to contemplate the destruction of his dad's lighthouse in the wake of defeat in the Civil War (1861-65). He was struggling to buy back his Black Banks plantation and restore it to some semblance of a working farm. However, Gould's son, Horace Jr., would soon find himself working in the burgeoning timber industry, which would bank on Georgia's tall pines to resurrect Coastal Georgia to new economic heights.

The demand for that timber would attract sailing ships from up and down the coast and around the world. And those ships would need a light to guide their path to St. Simons Island and to the Port of Brunswick.

By this time, Orlando Poe was Chief Engineer for the United States Lighthouse Board. As such, he designed the St. Simons Lighthouse. (Similar structures subsequently built on the Great Lakes are known today at "Poe Lighthouses.")

The builder of this new lighthouse was renowned architect Charles Cluskey, whose earlier Greek revival style work included the Governor's Mansion in Milledgeville and the Medical College of Georgia in Augusta. Cluskey served as construction contractor on this job.

Congress allocated the $45,000 for the lighthouse by 1867, but the contract was not awarded to Cluskey until the fall of 1869. Work was slowed in the steamy summer months of 1870 by malaria, which was thought at the time to arise from foul air in the swampy marshes. Folks were still about 20 years away from discovering it was those dang mosquitos all along.

And Malaria most likely was the culprit that struck down Cluskey, who died in 1871 before the project's completion. The lighthouse and keeper's dwelling were completed a year later in 1872.

The keeper's dwelling was a two-story structure, designed to house the keeper and his assistant. By 1880, lighthouse keeper Frederick Osborne and his family lived on the main floor and assistant John Stephens and his family lived on the top floor. Each floor had direct access to the lighthouse steps, with Osborne and Stephens entrusted with the formidable task of keeping the lighthouse oil lamp lit 24/7, 365.

It must have been cramped quarters for the men and their families. The day came when Stephens felt his wife's honor needed defending against a perceived slight from his boss. Osborne did not suffer Stephens' grievance modestly. An argument ensued.

Stephens shot Osborne, fatally wounding him. Stephens later beat the murder rap, acquitted by a jury at trial in Brunswick. The ghost of Osborne is said to preside at the lighthouse still today. The whole specter spectrum — footsteps, apparitions, supernatural suspense. A ghost tale from 1908 has it that the phantom of Osborne aided a light keeper's wife by fixing a glitch in the works one dark and stormy night.

But you don't need a penchant for the paranormal to see the St. Simons Lighthouse as possibly our most relevant and tangible living link to the Golden Isles' storied past. It has served as a constant beacon in the night sky for some 145 years without fail, shining a continuous guiding light out into the Atlantic Ocean — from the time of 19th Century sailing ships right up to the massive turbo-charged diesel freighters that will ply the St. Simons Sound to the Port of Brunswick this very day.

And while the lighthouse has gone from oil to electric to automated over the decades and centuries, the 7-foot-tall French-designed rotating crystal lens that Poe put atop it way back when remains the same.

In addition to being an official Coast Guard Aid to Navigation, the lighthouse is a living museum dedicated to schooling us on our past. The St. Simons Lighthouse Museum has been under the direction of the Coastal Georgia Historical Society since 1975.

Pay them a visit ($12 for adults, $5 for kids) at 610 Beachview Drive, adjacent to beautiful Neptune Park. The spiraling, 129-step journey to the top will reward you with a panoramic vista of the island and the Atlantic that is not to be missed.

Igbo Landing
a defiant act for freedom

They were captured in Africa and hauled across the ocean against their will, eventually arriving in chains to the shores of St. Simons Island.

They may have been deemed mere chattel by the whites who bought them. You could call them prisoners of what is possibly the most brutish and shameful trade enterprise in human history. Bondsmen? Perhaps.

But these proud people of the west African Igbo tribe were not slaves. Oh, no — they were never slaves.

Rather than submit to an existence of bondage and forced labor at the hands of another, these products of proud warrior stock made a staggeringly poignant declaration of independence with their very lives. It happened right here in the Golden Isles, way back in May of 1803. Some 13 members of the Igbo tribe walked as one in chains into St. Simons Island's Dunbar Creek. Then and there, they drowned themselves rather than accept a life of enslavement.

This striking testament to the harsh legacy of slavery is revered and preserved within the local African American community. It also is a much-cherished story among their descendants back in the Igbo homeland in present day southeastern Nigeria. But there is little in the way of a public marker here on St. Simons Island to commemorate the Igbo's resolve to live free or die. That seems a shame. Their sacrifice embodies the distinctly American traits of independence, self-determination and, when forced, strong-arm rebellion in the name of freedom. Thus, they are due a reverent place in the hearts and minds of all Americans.

Chieftains of the Igbo tribe came to St. Simons Island on July 22 in 2017 from their tribal homeland in Nigeria to pay homage to these distant kinsfolks, who died alone in a strange land so many generations past. These visiting dignitaries consecrated

Igbo elder Chief Dozie Ikedife came from Nigeria in 2017 to break bread with the tribe's distant relatives on Dunbar Creek. (Photo: Bobby Haven)

the ground and paid tribute to their relatives with a ceremonial breaking of a native Kola nut.

"We value and recognize our dead," explained Nigerian native Bobby Aniekwu, an attorney in Atlanta whose more formal title is Igbo Chieftain. "Those who drowned may be still restless, so we have come to renew our ties with them and, through us, with their homeland. We must, because we believe they are always with us."

The Igbo people claim ties to the tribes of Israel through the lineage of Gad, the seventh son of Jacob, Aniekwu explained. Their heritage is one of courage, fortitude and the unexstinguishable spark within the human spirit.

Indeed, the Igbo (sometimes referred to as Ebo) had gained a reputation throughout the slave-holding South for being virulently resistant to attempts at subjugation.

The story of Ebo (Igbo) Landing begins in Savannah, with the arrival directly from Africa of captives from that tribe. Mostly fact and part legend, versions of the journey from there vary somewhat. Approximately 75 of them were sold in 1803 at auction in Savannah, acquired for the plantations of John Couper on St. Simons Island and Thomas Spalding on Sapelo Island.

They were loaded upon the small sailing ship Morovia, bound first for Sapelo Island. By most accounts, however, the Igbo rebelled against the ship's crewmen, who were either thrown or jumped overboard to their deaths. Aniekwu says Igbo history holds there were three crewman who were overpowered in what might be among America's first slave revolts.

"This story is very well-known back home," said Aniekwu, whose duties call him back there several times a year.

Regardless of its original destination, the Morovia came ashore in Dunbar Creek on St. Simons Island. It is there that a contingent of the captives went into the water in chains and drowned. Roswell King, a white overseer on Pierce Butler's St. Simons Island plantation, stood witness to the macabre scene. He related that the Igbo "took to the swamp" and drowned rather than face a life in chains.

There is strong evidence to support this version of the events, eagerly supported by the island's ghost tour guides.

As tradition has it, those chains made an eerie accompaniment to their dying chant as they followed a tribal leader into the river: "The Water Spirit brought us, the Water Spirit will take us home."

In fact, generations of African American oral history speak of the defiant act as one of reverent salvation, not of death. Igbo spiritual traditions of the time inform us that they simply went home, returning by the waters from whence they came. These Igbo were captured in the area of present-day Nigeria's Umballa River, upon which they were transported to the coast for the transatlantic journey, Aniekwu explains. Their sad odyssey ended on Dunbar Creek, a river of sorts on Georgia's Coast.

"They were thinking, *We came by a river, and a river is going to take us home*," he said.

A new twist in Neptune Small's story only strengthens legacy

W ell, it appears as if the true-life storybook tale of our beloved Neptune Small is not entirely true.

But, if anything, the story gets even better. The narrative still flows the same, except when you get to the happy-ending part. You know, that part we all know so well? The part where the King family of St. Simons Island's Retreat Plantation granted their former slave a portion of land in gratitude for his devotion?

Heck, it is all right there on a plaque in the ground in the county park that bears his name beside the island's Pier Village. Although born enslaved, Neptune was the lifelong friend and servant of Retreat's Henry Lord King. The two were born just months apart in 1831. When Lord King was killed at the Battle of Fredericksburg during the Civil War, Neptune retrieved his friend's body from the horrific battlefield and brought him home. And then ...

"After the war the King family gave this portion of Retreat Plantation to Neptune ...," the plaque at the county park reads.

Except that is not what happened. There is no indication that Neptune ever owned any of the land on which Neptune Park now sits. Nor is there any evidence the Kings ever gave Neptune any property. Neptune's story of heroism and unconditional love necessarily, and rightfully, evokes lyrical prose and dramatic storytelling.

But the truth is written in the tedious legalese of land titles and deeds, dating back to the 1880s. King descendant Ed MacKethan came across the truth while researching property records for a book he prepared on Retreat Plantation eight years ago. His conclusion?

"No record of any land sale or transfer from the King family

Renowned local sculptor Kevin Pullen's depiction of Neptune Small with Lord King's body. (Photo: Bobby Haven)

to him has been found, and (there is) no evidence of Neptune Small's having owned any of the land that is Neptune Park," MacKethan writes in his report.

But perhaps Neptune did not need anybody's help or hand-outs, according to Glynn County property records. Neptune the freedman was a landowner in his own right. On Oct. 17, 1884, Neptune bought eight acres on St. Simons Island for $102 from James P. Keaton, according to records. Neptune's spread was located somewhere in the area of present-day Neptune Way and Park Avenue, several blocks west of where Neptune Park now sits.

"No indication has been found of how Neptune Small obtained the $102 cost other than from his own funds," MacKethan wrote.

While the Kings were no doubt grateful to Neptune for his epic struggle, they likely were in no condition financially in the war's aftermath to bequeath such a gift, MacKethan speculates. Mallery King, the King family patriarch at the time, was selling off Retreat land just to stay afloat.

So, how does this revelation affect the overall storyline of this favored piece of local lore? One thing does not change. Neptune was the best friend that the rich and privileged Lord ever had. It was common in Antebellum times for a family to designate a child born enslaved as servant and companion to a child of the plantation family. By all accounts, the bond between Lord and Neptune was uncommonly strong.

When Lordy, as he was known, joined the Confederate Army as an officer, Neptune accompanied him. He cooked his meals and cleaned his clothes, among other duties. By December of 1862, Lordy was an officer in the Confederate Army in Fredericksburg, Va. Neptune was there, too.

The Battle of Fredericksburg delivered a tremendous victory for the South, but it brought heartache to the King family. Lordy volunteered for a reconnaissance mission that took him outside Confederate lines. He did not return.

Neptune ventured out to find him in the no-man's land of dead and dying between the Union and Confederate lines. Crawling over bodies as gunfire still cracked though the night air, Neptune finally found Lordy's body and carried him from the field. With

Lordy in a pine coffin loaded on a wagon, Neptune then began his old friend's long, sad journey home.

Leaving his wife Ila and baby daughter at home, Neptune then returned to the warfront in the service of Lordy's younger brother, Richard Cuyler, who was fighting with a battalion in Georgia and Tennessee.

It is all there. Friendship. Devotion. Tragedy. Heartache. Sacrifice. Struggle. Redemption. And then we get to the heartwarming part, where the Kings give Neptune a piece of their land to call his very own. But property records of the day tell us otherwise. I am not the first history writer to get it wrong, although I did repeat the inaccuracy in my little book with the big title: "A Historical Crash Course on Coastal Georgia and the Golden Isles."

Donna Shrum pointed it out to me in a very nice email some months back. The teacher and freelance writer from Virginia had come upon the truth while researching an article about Neptune for Georgia Backroads Magazine (A very good read). MacKethan's research is kept in the archives at the St. Simons Island Lighthouse Museum, she informed me.

I thanked Shrum but told her I would have to confirm the facts independently when I could find time. I later made an appointment with the museum's always-helpful curator, Mimi Rogers.

The truth has been hiding in plain sight, right there in Glynn County's 19th century property records. In fact, Neptune even made an earlier purchase of 13 acres in Brunswick, for which he paid $78, according to those records.

At war's end, Lordy was laid to rest at Christ Church on St. Simons Island. Neptune lovingly tended his graveside for years.

But Neptune also moved on, as the new evidence indicates. He had four children with Ila before her death in the 1870s. Neptune had two more children with his second wife, Charlotte Galery. A self-made man and a property owner, his final years served as an example to this community of freedom's true value.

He lived a full rewarding life right up until his death in 1907. And that happy ending deserves to live on in our cherished memories.

Island dispatches from the rambunctious 19th century

I t has since evolved into one of St. Simons Island's better ghost stories, but back in March of 1880 the shooting of the lighthouse keeper by his assistant was breaking news.

"On Sunday morning, at about 8:30, an unfortunate occurrence transpired at St. Simons Light House, in which Mr. Fred Osborne was seriously shot by his assistant, Mr. John W. Stevens."

So wrote Dr. R.J. Massey, St. Simons Island's roving reporter for the *Brunswick Advertiser*, the weekly newspaper of record at the time. The above dispatch appeared in the March 6 edition of the *Advertiser* (later the *Advertiser and Appeal*). By the time the next edition came out a week later, Massey reported just how seriously Osborne was shot.

"Frederick Osborne, who was shot in the Stevens-Osborne tragedy, an account of which we gave last week, died last Wednesday at 3:30 p.m."

Tales of Osborne's disgruntled ghost stalking the 104-foot tower's 129 winding steps are a favorite, spun stylishly by today's local ghost tour operators. Like any good reporter who knows his chops, Massey stuck to the facts as they unfolded in 1880. Massey recounts in the March 6 article the disagreement that led to Osborne and Stevens adjourning "into the bushes in front of the (lightkeeper's) house to settle their difficulty. During this interview Stevens threatened to chastise Osborne, when Osborne drew his pistol and ordered him not to advance further, whereupon Stevens went back into the house, took down his double-barreled shot gun … "

Massey goes on to note that Stevens was loaded for deer — buckshot. As Osborne pressed forward down a nearby path, Stevens let him have it "at a distance of 98 feet, hitting him in four places, only one shot, however, taking serious effect."

It was not all blood and guts on Massey's St. Simons Island beat. That same month our faithful scribe engaged in some unabashed boosterism for the timber industry that drove the local economy back then.

"We have the assurance of Capt. Hunt that the timber now being sent by the St. Simons Mills to New York Elevated Railway is as fine a lot of timber as there is in the world," he wrote. "That there is not even a possibility of a flaw in any single piece."

Nor was Massey above performing a playful public service: "Our clever and efficient telegraph operator, Cornelius Casey, found a pocket book the other day. By identifying it, the owner can have it and all the money thereunto belonging."

Dang, I love the way a wordsmith of the late 19th Century could turn a phrase. These vintage news nuggets were gleaned from "Pages From the Past, St. Simons Island 1880-1886." Compiled by Beth Engel and Geneva Stebbins from the newspaper collections of renowned local historian Margaret Davis Cate, this 112-page treasure was published in 1975 on the Jesup Sentinel press.

This edition was graciously loaned out to me from the collection of Bill Brown, the Golden Isles' prolific nonagenarian and living local history museum.

As a lifelong newspaperman, I find Massey's reports particularly enjoyable. His dispatches began a full two decades before *The Brunswick News* first established itself as the paper of record in 1902, and nearly 140 years before I would have the honor of chronicling the doings hereabouts.

Massey began his local newspaper career with a much more impressive resume than I could ever hope to attain. The "Dr." preceding his name was no mere academic decoration. Dr. R.J. Massey's day job was as a practicing physician and surgeon in the island community of St. Simons Mills.

His weekly column covering current events on St. Simons became a mainstay of *The Advertiser* from 1880 to '86, at which time he moved to the mainland and retired from both medicine and media. His reports and musings provide a revealing glimpse at the island, in a completely different place and time.

Twilight turtle walks of the day were strenuous affairs that could work up an appetite. The faint of heart need not apply. "On Tuesday night about 10 o'clock as Mr. Wm. Gowne and lady were taking a moonlight ride upon the beach, they observed a large loggerhead turtle emerge from the water and make for the bank," he reported. "Mr. G. tackled him and after much exertion ... succeeded in turning him on his back. He was then brought up and butchered. Not a bad night's find by any means."

Tales of armed encounters with wildlife abound, including accounts of islanders gunning down everything from rattlesnakes to wildcats, deer and alligators.

But tourism was already emerging as an economic boon, as evidenced in this call for investment in a seaside motel.

"It would prove a healthful summer resort ... whilst it would be equally popular as a (winter) wayside house for the Northern tourist to spend a month ... "

For Island's African American community, there are no strangers at Union Memorial

Amy Roberts' footing struggled on a September morning with the uneven soggy ground beneath her, and occasional breezes shook loose the previous night's leftover raindrops from the pine needles overhead.

This tangled patch off an unbeaten path is about as close to the middle of nowhere as you will find these days on St. Simons Island. Sure, the second-story eaves of million-dollar homes in a nearby subdivision hover on the western horizon, but you cannot get here from there.

In fact, a person driving by on the pair of tire tracks through high grass that passes for a road back here might not see Union Memorial Cemetery for the forest that resides within it. But this is hallowed ground for folks like Roberts, members of the island's deeply-rooted African American community. And so should it be for us all.

Buried here in this wooded lot surrounded by hurricane fencing is a treasure of local history and lore. Reliable teachers, merchants and war veterans from the early 20th century lie at rest beside a woman who once sang at Carnegie Hall and branches from the family tree of one of the NFL's all-time greats. And for all that is known here, the many unmarked graves scattered throughout Union Memorial speak of more history still to be rediscovered.

These aging gravestones tucked into the woods off Demere Road beg for spooky ghost tales, but Roberts ambles around the cemetery with the good cheer of a first cousin at a family picnic. The deceased she does not know personally, she knows by heritage.

Bessie Jones of the famed Georgia Sea Island Singers is among those buried at Union Memorial.

She points out the grave of Nora P. Daughtry (1888-1951), the aunt of legendary NFL running back Jim Brown, who spent his childhood on St. Simons Island. And over there is the headstone for Bessie S. Jones (1902-1954), star of the famed Georgia Sea Island Singers, who performed at Carnegie, Central Park and at folk festivals from Newport to the Smithsonian.

A short stroll leads to the markers for Adrian H. Johnson (1907-74) and Luetta B. Johnson (1914-77), the couple who were the last educators at the island's Harrington School. Those buried among them are people who served this country's military, ranging from a Korean War veteran all the way back to Ceasar Johnson (1900-60), a private in the army during World War I.

"There is so much history out here," said Roberts, Executive Director of the St. Simons Island African American Heritage Coalition.

The history of Union Memorial Cemetery by necessity is tied to the slave days of the Antebellum period in the Golden Isles. The cemetery also is known as Strangers Cemetery. These so-called "strangers" were blacks who arrived after the Civil War. Beginning in the 1870s, these freedmen went to work in the saw-mills that sprouted near present-day Gascoigne Park.

The "strangers" were so-called to differentiate them from the descendants of those enslaved on the island's sprawling cotton plantations — Retreat, Black Banks and St. Clar, among them. Those recently emancipated from St. Simons Island plantations still held hereditary rights to be buried in their family plantation's cemeteries.

"If you were not associated with the plantations, you could not be buried on the plantation," Roberts explained, walking among the headstones. "You had to be buried here, at Union, because you were a stranger."

And here we come to one of those quirky time warps where past and present blend. Union Memorial is no quaint outdoor museum piece, but a cemetery that is still open for business. So too are those black cemeteries with ties to the plantation era. Local descendants of those once enslaved on plantations can choose to be buried at those ancestral cemeteries.

Roberts holds strong historical interest in Union Memorial, but her family is no "stranger" to St. Simons Island. She plans to be laid to rest at Retreat Cemetery, as is her birthright. She will rest beside her parents, sister and grandmother at the cemetery, which is on the grounds of Sea Island's Retreat Golf Course off Kings Way.

Before the ink dried on my notes about this, Roberts points out the resting place of her brother, James Lotson. Lotson was an Army veteran, once decorated by Gen. Dwight D. Eisenhower for driving a flaming supply truck out of harm's way. But Lotson chose the secluded grounds of Union Memorial over the present country club setting at Retreat.

"He did not want golf balls landing on his head," Roberts said, smiling.

About this time, James Williams strode up to Roberts and handed her the walking stick she left behind in her parked car. She did not even have to ask him. A gentleman and a Vietnam War army veteran, Williams plans one day in the way distant future to rest in the tidy family plot at Union Memorial, beside his mother, father and others.

"This to me represents the slave peoples who went on to create for themselves the American dream," Williams said.

Prominent black newspaper publisher's descendants foster his legacy locally

obert S. Abbott rose to prominence in the early 20th century as a powerful newspaper publisher and a champion of racial equality, establishing himself as one of America's first black millionaires in the process.

But the publisher of *The Chicago Defender* never forgot his humble ties to St. Simons Island. That devotion endures still today in the form of a stately obelisk that stands on the grounds of Fort Frederica National Monument. That obelisk is a tribute, in part, to Abbott's biological father, Thomas Abbott. That same land had previously encompassed portions of Capt. Charles Stevens' Oatland Plantation, where Thomas Abbott was born into slavery.

Robert Abbott also was born on St. Simons Island, in 1868 — some three years after the Civil War's end effectively eradicated the stain of slavery in the U.S. However, Abbott's skin color exposed him early and often to prejudice, galvanizing his commitment to waging a vigorous war of words against racial injustice from the pulpit of his nationally-circulated newspaper.

His rise to prominence as one of America's most influential black men is chock full of intrigue, inspiration, struggle and triumph. It is a tale that involves enough plot twists and cliffhangers to fuel a Netflix viewing binge.

Fortunately, it is a story that folks like LaTanya Abbott Austin know by heart, and never tire of retelling.

"He's my great-granduncle," LaTanya said recently. "They credited him and his newspaper with the Great Northern Migration. He was an amazing man, very courageous. His whole message was about uniting mankind with love and peace. He was

LaTanya Abbott Austin is the great grandniece of black newspaper publisher Robert S. Abbott. (Photo: Bobby Haven)

way ahead of his time."

One of many direct descendants of the Abbott line who live locally, LaTanya also is an active member of the Robert S. Abbott Race Unity Institute. The local group meets regularly to foster racial and spiritual harmony among people of diverse backgrounds; all are welcome to join (theabbottinstitute.org).

Race, skin color and the senseless prejudices attached to the kaleidoscope of variations of the human condition perplexed Robert Abbott from an early age. He was born after all, the son of a black former slave and later raised by a mixed-race stepfather. And though he never knew his birth father, Robert Abbott never forgot his roots or the island from which they sprouted.

Following the Civil War, Thomas Abbott took his newfound freedom and moved to Savannah. There he met and married Flora Butler, a hairdresser at the Savannah Theater. The couple soon returned to St. Simons Island, where Robert Abbott was born. Thomas Abbott would die of tuberculosis within a year of his son's birth.

Thomas was buried with full recognition in the Stevens' family cemetery, an indication of the love and respect the family held for him. Flora returned with her young son to Savannah, where she met and married John Sengstacke. Sengstacke was the bi-racial son of a German sea captain and a former slave, Tara. Herman Sengstacke had bought Tara out of slavery in Savannah.

John Sengstacke bequeathed his middle name to his stepson, thus the S. in Robert S. Abbott. As an educator and editor of the little Woodville Times, published outside of Savannah, John Sengstacke might also be credited with instilling in Robert Abbott his love of newspapering.

One thing Robert inherited from his biological father was a rich ebony complexion. It would make him a target of racial prejudice throughout his life, beginning with his higher education. While attending Hampton College in Virginia, Robert confided to a white teacher and mentor his inexplicable bewilderment over the irrational concept of judging folks solely on skin color.

"I told him, among other things, that I could not understand why there should be so much prejudice," he is quoted as saying in his biography, Lonely Warrior.

Robert would go on to earn a degree from Chicago's Kent College of Law, where he was the only black person in his class. But Robert never got the chance to prove himself as a lawyer. At the time, "his dark skin tone was too much of an impediment," his biography states.

After struggling to make ends meet in Chicago with occasional print work, Robert launched The Chicago Defender in 1904. With an investment of just two bits, the Defender's first edition was produced in his landlord's kitchen. Despite many a detractor's prediction to the contrary, the Chicago Defender became the voice of black America. The paper had a circulation of more than 200,000 in several states by 1920.

The Defender made its way into Deep South states via the black porters on Pullman railroad cars. The paper unflinchingly exposed details of the savage racially-motivated lynchings of that era. It promoted Chicago and other northern cities as a place where blacks could realize the American dream.

As historian Lawrence D. Hogan noted in 1984, Abbott "was the pioneer for the Negro press as Hearst was for the White metropolitan press."

Sometime in the 1930s, Robert S. Abbott returned to St. Simons Island for the first time since he was a baby. He was here to christen the obelisk, placed over his father's grave in the old Stevens family cemetery. He spent $1,600 on the monument, which also honors his aunt Celia Abbott.

Robert had stayed in contact with family members here, lavishing many nieces and nephews with higher education and European vacations. Robert's commitment to magnanimity toward all people was evidenced in his relations with the Stevens family, the white folks who had once enslaved his father. During the tough times of the Depression, he assisted the Stevens' descendants financially and contributed to their grandchildren's education.

As historical writer Bruce W. Whitmore noted: "In other words, his life mirrored what he so often preached in the pages of The Defender: we must all learn to live together in unity and friendship."

Millie Wilcox preserves Island's history through mother's artwork, and not just a little Southern charm

Spend 30 minutes talking about St. Simons Island history with Millie Wilcox and you quickly realize that 30 hours would hardly suffice to gain her insight on the subject.

But half an hour is all Millie had to spare this day on her crowded calendar, so 30 minutes it was. We met midmorning at Mildred Huie Mediterranean House Plantation Museum, 1819 Frederica Road on St. Simons Island. The museum features the captivating paintings of Millie's late mother, Mildred Huie (1906-2000). Mildred held an abiding love of St. Simons Island history, which comes to life in a kaleidoscope of colors on canvass, covering virtually every wall in every room inside the museum.

Mildred's paintings depict the plantations of St. Simons Island's Antebellum period, churches from its storied past, Fort Frederica and early settlements, as well as the simple pastoral traditions of a bygone island era. A painting covering an entire wall directly across from the museum's entrance serves as a map to the past. It depicts the entire island and all its landmarks from those distant days.

A painting may be worth a thousand words, but Millie has far more details than such brevity could contain on each and every painting displayed within. But this is just a 30-minute visit, she reminds me, so there is little time to waste. We remove several ink drawings from one end of a couch, and Millie begins a history lesson mixed with fact, fancy and lots of charm.

I ask first about her connection to the island. Millie came to St. Simons Island from Albany, Ga., by way of Italy. "I was in the fashion business," the Georgia belle says. And it all makes perfect sense. (She graduated from the University of Georgia,

Millie Wilcox, with art by her late mother, Mildred Huie.

then gravitated from the fashion industry hubs of New York City to those in Rome before moving here full-time in the 1960s, I later learn).

Millie's family in Albany were frequent visitors to St. Simons Island going back to her childhood. Millie would later serve as president of the St. Simons Island Chamber of Commerce, marry island hotelier Robert Wilcox, and become the proprietor of The Left Bank Art Gallery until 2017.

The Mediterranean-style home that houses the museum was built in 1929 by engineer Fred Stroberg. A canal once ran beside the house, which sat in front of the old Redfern airfield. "Fred would fly his plane in to Redfern, walk to his boathouse, and take his boat out into the water," Millie said.

She goes on to talk about everything from her mom's friendship with local historic romance novelist Eugenia Price to the deadly Hazzard/Wylly feud to "frizzle chickens." Frizzle chickens had curled feathers, pointing inward instead of outward. Gullah-Geechee traditions hold that frizzle chickens were good to have around; these birds could scratch out any hex an enemy might plant in your yard. Mildred Huie was fascinated by frizzle chickens, featuring them often in her paintings, Millie said.

Great, I said, but let's back up. Did you mention a feud? On St. Simons? And something about a pink chapel? A sparkle glints in Millie's eye. She had informed me at the offset that history's anecdotal sidetracks often intrigue her more than the march of time's overall narrative.

"I think that is one of the most interesting anecdotes," Millie said.

Dr. Thomas Fuller Hazzard was a son of Col. William Hazzard, a Revolutionary War veteran from South Carolina. In 1818, Hazzard bought the West Point Plantation, located north of then-abandoned Fort Frederica. West Point then went to Hazzard's oldest son, Col. William Wigg Hazzard. Enter the younger brother, Dr. Thomas Fuller Hazzard. He bought the adjacent property, Pike's Bluff.

On the other side of the brewing feud, John Wylly acquired The Village Plantation, which was next to Pike's Bluff. The Wyllys and the Hazzards both were faithful congregants at Christ Church.

The Hazzard brothers were quite popular, avid journal keepers and recorders of local history. They enjoyed a bracing hunt with good hounds, had a keen eye for quality horses and owned the racing boats Shark and Comet.

Despite all that expanse of land between plantations back then, John Wylly and Thomas Hazzard could not amicably resolve a squabble that arose regarding their common property line. The two agreed that only a deadly duel with pistols could settle the matter, complete with white cloth pinned to each man's shirt targeting the heart.

Such a dramatic standoff never happened. Instead, the two crossed paths at a gathering at Brunswick's original Oglethorpe Hotel on Dec. 3, 1838.

Words escalated. Wylly gave Hazzard a rap with his cane. Hazzard drew a pistol and shot Wylly in the heart, killing him instantly. A jury later acquitted Hazzard of manslaughter, but island neighbors and fellow Christ Church members returned a less-forgiving verdict.

Ostracized, the Hazzard family built their small "chapel of ease" at West Point. The pink hue the tabby walls later assumed probably resulted from lichen growth. In the spinning of a good St. Simons Island ghost tale, however, that pink naturally became the blood on Hazzard's hands.

Note: Millie's museum closed its door in early 2018.

Woman devoted life to singing Geechee's praises, preserving unique musical heritage

Julia Armstrong's lyrical singing as she went about her housework struck a pleasing chord with Lydia Parrish, those distinctly African rhythms transporting the lady of the house back to her Quaker childhood in New England.

The setting was St. Simons Island, probably around 1915. Armstrong was a member of St. Simons' Geechee community, descendants of coastal plantation slaves whose ancestors managed through generations of bondage to preserve and endow legacies of their African roots. Parrish was the child of abolitionist Quakers, whose community in Salem County, N.J., had welcomed blacks seeking a new life after escaping bondage in the South.

It was the beginning of a beautiful relationship.

From it came the preservation of musical traditions unique to the Gullah-Geechee culture here. That music would take flight to broader acclaim and, in the process, result in Parrish's book, *Slave Songs of the Georgia Sea Islands*. The music would play to adoring international audiences through the Georgia Sea Island Singers. Renowned folk artist and St. Simons Islander Bessie Jones would go on to perform it at Carnegie Hall and at music festivals from Newport to the Smithsonian.

One song preserved through her book, "Pay Me My Money Down," has long been a staple at Bruce Springsteen concerts. It is credited to Lydia, but the real authors of this jab at overbearing foremen were 19th Century black stevedores from right here in the Golden Isles.

These local African musical roots persevere still today, from the joyous cacophony of a ring-shout performance in McIntosh County to the funky vibes of a new band on the American music scene called Ranky Tanky.

Lydia was married to famed painter/illustrator Maxfield Parrish, who was among the most well-known American artists of his time. By the time she began wintering on St. Simons Island at the turn-of-the-century, estranged is likely the best word to describe their matrimony.

But back to Salem County, N.J. Lydia was born Lydia Amber Austin in 1872. Many blacks who escaped slavery had long been settled among the abolitionist-minded Quakers, bringing with them a seemingly inherent musical tradition that was not of this continent or of the Old World.

"The slave songs that Parrish heard echoing from the kitchen and the fields in her home community touched a part of her that she believed Victorian strictures had suppressed," historian Melissa Cooper writes in her book, *Making Gullah: A History of Sapelo Islanders, Race, and the American Imagination*.

In other words, Lydia could dig it.

Lydia and Maxfield Parrish married in 1895 and settled into the artsy Cornish Colony, a New Hampshire community of broad-minded creative types. While Lydia raised their four children, Maxfield's romantic interests turned to one of his young models.

Whatever Lydia thought of this, the marriage held. She soon began taking her summers on St. Simons Island. Her home was on property near the present big bend on Old Demere Road; it was once part of the Kelvin Grove Plantation.

And that is where Julia Armstrong's sweet singing first took Lydia home to the beloved music of her childhood.

"She heard Julia singing one day and she was captivated," said Sudy Leavy, a Lydia Parrish buff and long-time St. Simons Islander. Leavy has done much research on Lydia, and at one time portrayed her in historical skits at the St. Simons Lighthouse Museum. "She got her to sing some of the old songs," said Leavy, who now lives in Athens. "Those were the songs she heard in her youth."

But the Geechee were reluctant to share their music with whites or outsiders, according to accounts. The detailed explanations for this are many, varied and laden with academia that

Lydia Parrish's book helped preserve the unique sound of the Georgia Sea Islands.

could consume the entire space allotted for this column. Basically, Lydia proved to the Geechee that she truly loved the music. She made friends in the Geechee community. She paid to hear performances, a practice that musicians have long valued.

By 1920, Lydia had helped form the Spiritual Singers Society of Coastal Georgia. This was the forerunner of the Georgia Sea Island Singers that would include the renowned Bessie Jones, Mabel Hillary and Joe Armstrong, the husband of Julie. Over the next couple of decades, Lydia catalogued songs passed down in memory from Africa to the Georgia Coast, taking care to document the vital connections in the process. An amateur folklorist, Lydia had considerable help from respected folklorist Alan Lomax and America's first black linguist, Lorenzo Dow Turner.

Her book includes transcripts from the daily journal of Mohammad Bilali, the literate slave and plantation overseer at Thomas Spalding's Sapelo plantation. The chapter titled "African Survivals on the Coast of Georgia" is devoted to Geechee songs with direct African ties and dialects.

"Fifteen years into her career as a preservationist .... Lydia Parrish began a relentless quest to prove that the slave songs she collected and the ring shout performances she observed were definitive evidence of African survivals in America," the historian Cooper writes.

It was a quest that also was a labor of love.

Redfern: An almost historic name, this pilot's final flight was launched from Sea Island

On the early afternoon of Aug. 25, 1927, a young barnstormer sat in the cockpit of his Stinson SM-1 Detroiter at a Sea Island airstrip, poised to make the words Brunswick and Redfern as synonymous with triumph in the skies as St. Louis and Lindberg.

Paul Redfern was a 25-year-old pilot from South Carolina. His colorful trek to this historic moment was typical of the foolhardy heroes who ventured up there in the infancy of human flight. Redfern's plan was to take off from the Georgia Coast in his monoplane christened "The Port of Brunswick" and fly nonstop to Rio de Janeiro in Brazil, an astounding stretch of more than 4,600 miles. The feat would shatter Charles Lindberg's epic trans-Atlantic flight from New York to Paris in the Spirit of St. Louis earlier that year by a good thousand miles.

The plane was crammed with spare fuel tanks for the estimated 52-hour flight, cruising at about 85 mph at 5,000 feet. His view of the skies ahead of him was limited to a dinky periscope poking out of the fuselage; Redfern did have side windows to see what was passing. No radio on board, no fancy altimeter, Redfern had only a compass and a map to guide him.

The journey would take him first over endless miles of the Atlantic Ocean, followed by a marathon trek over untamed Amazon jungle. He carried a rifle, fish hooks and flares in case of an emergency landing, as well baubles to hopefully appease the head-hunting natives he might expect to encounter.

He took off in the heart of hurricane season, way before radar storm-tracking's advanced warning. The moon's cycle had run its course, meaning he would have no moonlight at nighttime to help guide him.

Paul Redfern

Some 3,000 folks gathered at the airstrip on Sea Island to see him off, including his loving wife, Gertrude. She put up a good front, smiling confidently at her husband as he hopped in the plane for this perilous adventure. Accounts say Gertrude broke down and sobbed in the arms of a bystander as soon as Redfern's plane disappeared in the Coastal Georgia skies shortly after his 12:46 p.m. takeoff.

In case you did not already know, or have not figured it out yet, things did not end well for Redfern. He was never heard from again.

The most credible last sighting of Redfern came the next day over Ciudad Bolivar in Venezuela, where an American engineer claimed he saw The Port of Brunswick "trailing a thin wisp of black smoke." Witness Lee Dennison said he could read the plane's identifying tail number.

Earlier that day Redfern descended on the Norwegian ship Christian Krohg some 200 miles offshore from the port of La Guaira, dropping a message in a carton on the deck. The ship's crew somehow relayed to Redfern that he needed to keep flying due south to reach South America.

Disappointment greeted the hundreds who awaited his arrival in Rio de Janeiro, where President Washington Luis and silent movie diva Clara Bow were among the well-wishers.

This promotional stunt in the name of pushing flight's frontiers all started with Brunswick's Board of Trade, charged with attracting business to the port.

Lindberg flew across the Atlantic Ocean on May 20 of 1927 mainly because New York hotelier Raymond Orteig had ponied up a $25,000 jackpot for the first person who could do it. That was a whole lot of money in those days.

Brunswick's Board of Trade quickly came up with the idea of matching that reward, offering the money to any takers up for an airborne adventure from Georgia to Brazil. Board members hoped to put their city's deep-water port on the world map.

Redfern quickly answered the challenge, seizing the chance for fame, glory and riches. As a teenager in Columbia, S.C., the resourceful youngster fashioned his own glider out of cardboard and scraps, soaring "The World's Smallest Flying Machine" for a loop above a local cow field. A couple of years later, Redfern similarly contrived a bi-plane powered by a World War I plane's engine.

Redfern seems characteristic of the audacious pilots from that pioneering era, performing aerobatics above county fairs and stumping for businesses with aerial advertising. Redfern even used his plane to help the law track down moonshine stills. He himself was once arrested for doing a fly-by too close to the top of a moving train, even by the standards of rowdy Texans.

The Redfern Village shopping plaza on St. Simons Island is named for him, as is Redfern Drive on the island. An early air strip on St. Simons Island also was named for him. Likewise, Rio de Janeiro too has a street named Redfern.

And there are many who believe Redfern descendants exist somewhere in between. Some experts lent significant credibility to reports streaming out of the jungle in the years following his failed flight that Redfern survived a crash with only some broken bones. Reports that he was adopted by friendly natives and had taken a tribal wife sparked several expeditions over the next 10 years. All returned empty handed. But, hey, the Amazon is a mighty big place. Who knows?

Anyway, next time you are dining at one of those nice restaurants in the Redfern Village venue on St. Simons Island, be sure to give its namesake a toast with your mug of brew or your glass of sweet tea.

Hazel's Cafe endures today as a throwback to Island's past

An unpainted wooden shack sits charmingly out of place along Demere Road on St. Simons Island's south end, the burnt red of the rusted tin roof serving as its most colorful feature.

The weather-beaten sign nailed to the front gable explains everything, but for most passersby it only further twists the riddle behind this island anachronism. "Hazel's Cafe," it reads in waning block letters above the fading Coca-Cola logo.

Yet, after Amy Roberts walked inside and closed the door behind her Tuesday morning, it was the contemporary surroundings outside the old building that suddenly seemed out of step with the times.

"This was a jamming little place," Roberts mused, referring the community Hazel's Cafe once served. "There was a rooming house across the street, then there was the Jackson Apartments on other side of where that brick home is now. There were juke joints and Wilma's Theater, the Pavilion and the Atlantic Inn, which was down by the (St. Simons Elementary) school."

She paused in her reverie to answer my question.

"It was all African American, of course," she said.

Hazel and Thomas Floyd opened the cafe in 1947, banking on the post-war economic boom to generate business. Boy, did it. Hazel's Cafe already was an iconic relic when it finally closed its doors to customers in 1978, some 40 years ago.

Thomas was from Hazelhurst, arriving on St. Simons Island after serving in the Army during World War II (1941-45). He was a darned good cook. Hazel was an island native, ready for a change of pace after having worked in Brunswick's Liberty Ship yards during the war years. Together, the couple whipped up a recipe for success that would feed the community for three de-

Established in 1947, Hazel's Café still stands along Demere Road.

cades.

They served mostly takeout dinners, but the place also had a dining area with tables and a bar inside. On weekends, they would fire up the outdoor cooking pit and serve barbecue. Hazel would go down to the St. Simons Island Pier and catch crabs, which she prepared for customers in a variety of ways.

The menu at Hazel's always pleased a clientele on the go. A lot of the folks worked in what is known today as the service industry — either at island resorts and hotels, or in private homes. Some worked also for local businesses, such as Fendig Signs, Amy said.

The cafe's original cash register sits in a corner by the front door, with its nickel sized manual punch buttons. The bar running along the wall beside it is still there too. "And that's the kitchen where they cooked all those fabulous meals," Amy said. "Look at it — it's all still the same. They made dinners and sandwiches, and on the weekends they would grill, have a low country boil, fix fried fish sandwiches, just whatever."

73

Amy ought to know. Hazel is a cousin on her mother's side. "I was coming around here since I was a baby, in the late '40s," Amy said. Years later, Amy once drove Thomas all the way down to Miami, where he worked for a spell helping out his sister at her barbecue joint. Thomas, you see, had a wooden leg and could not drive.

"I drove him down there and left the car, and rode the bus back up," Amy said. "He was a grill master, he used to cook before he went into the Army."

The cafe operated seven days a week. On Sundays, Hazel would start cooking early, then head down the road to Emanuel Baptist Church for the service before returning home to feed the afternoon dinner crowd, Amy recalls.

Little else exists from those days, although descendants of the folks who contributed to this thriving African American community still live in family homes scattered around the island's south end. The call to worship is still answered robustly each Sunday at Emanuel Baptist, as it has been since 1890.

And on college football Saturdays in the fall, a band of happy Georgia Bulldog fans infuse Hazel's Cafe with life once again. They are the guests of St. Simons Islander and diehard Dawg fan Fred Marrs.

"I bought the place in 1994," said Fred, owner of Pane in the Glass on Arnold Road near Ocean Boulevard. "We grill out back and have a lot of fun with it. Mainly, we just watch Georgia football."

Historic preservation was not foremost on Fred's mind when he bought the large plot that includes the cafe. He intended to move his business there, but new zoning rules nixed commercial use of the land. A daughter built a home on land behind the old cafe, and another daughter owns the land beside it. Restoring and reviving Hazel's pretty much became Fred's hobby.

"Most people would have just clear-cut the land," Mars said. "I kept Hazel's for me."

And although Fred is white, it turns out he has a familial connection to Hazel's. "My sister was his babysitter, and she lived just across the street," Amy said of her late sibling Phoebe.

That would be the house on Demere Road where the "Don't

74

Ask Won't Sell" sign is tacked boldly to a pole out front. A niece of Amy's now lives there.

"Miss Phoebe took care of me when I was a little boy. Her daughter Cheryl and I used to play together. Miss Phoebe said I told her once, I want to marry Cheryl," Fred said with a laugh.

Inside Hazel's Cafe, little has changed except for a couple of modest flat-screen television sets, a billiards table and some track lighting. The many black and white photos of the island's yesteryears include a portrait of the old proprietors, a handsome couple indeed.

The home Hazel and Thomas lived in remains standing next door, used today for storage. Fred intends for this little piece of the island's past to stand for a long time to come.

"It's going to be willed to my daughter and she said she's not going to do anything with it," Fred said. "It's just going to be Hazel's. It's one of those things you keep forever."

BRUNSWICK

Brunswick's Olde English roots remain through the centuries

For his service to King, Country and Gen. James Oglethorpe, Mark Carr received 1,000 acres of riverfront property, sometime around 1738. Carr planted tobacco on the land, which he named Plug Point.

And that, more or less, is how the city of Brunswick got its start.

Capt. Carr served with distinction in Oglethorpe's Marine Boat Company at Fort Frederica, which was established on St. Simons Island in 1736 as the first line of defense against the Spanish threat from Florida.

The settlement's original name was apparently a reference to the plugs of tobacco Carr produced from the land there, according to sharp local historians like Amy Hedrick, the keeper of Coastal Georgia Genealogy and History (glynngen.com). Carr's original farm sat roughly between present-day Dartmouth Street and First Avenue, along the Turtle River.

This land got the royal treatment in 1771, when the British colony of Georgia bought it from Carr and named it Brunswick. After centuries of repetition, the name of Glynn County's only municipality may ring common to some folks these days. But Brunswick is actually named for the home town of the royal family of King George II. George II (1683-1760) was ascended from the royal House of Hanover in Braunschweig (Brunswick) in present-day north-central Germany.

The original township was laid out in a series of 12 public

© 13518 Hanover Park, Brunswick, Ga

squares, a design for colonial living known as — you guessed it — the Oglethorpe Plan. Hanover Square, on Newcastle Street, exists in its entirety still today. Remnants of the other public squares are found throughout Historic Brunswick, including Queen Square, where Old City Hall now sits.

But back to the beginning. Shortly after the oh-so-British town of Brunswick was founded, the Americans revolted against the Mother Country in 1775. Most of the residents remained loyal to the crown. Having picked the losing side, many of these original residents retreated from Brunswick to reside abroad where the sun still shined on the British Empire.

Founders of the new American incarnation of Brunswick included the likes of Urbanus Dart (1801-83), the son of Revolutionary War soldier and patriot Cyrus Dart. Regardless of the townsfolk's new allegiances, they saw no need to change the names of Brunswick's old English references. Take a stroll or pedal through town today and see the street names for yourself: London, George, Prince, Gloucester, Newcastle and Dartmouth, among numerous others.

If these streets sound like they belong on an episode of PBS's Downton Abbey, it is no mere coincidence. Even Union Street was named to commemorate the 1603 union of England and Scotland. Brunswick might have said good riddance to the tyrannical British monarchy, but they stayed true to their anglophile hearts with street and place names.

Shortly after independence was gained, Glynn Academy was founded in 1788. The city's high school is the second oldest in Georgia, behind only Richmond Academy in Richmond County.

And by 1789, President George Washington himself had established Brunswick's natural open water port as one of five Ports of Entry into the young nation. The others were New York, Baltimore, Philadelphia, and Boston.

Brunswick's beautiful port was problematic from a local commerce standpoint, however, being as it emptied into a marsh. Darien's comparatively lousy port connected to the Altamaha River, which served as a natural delivery route for cotton and other inland trade goods and agricultural products.

But some of Brunswick's local movers and shakers devised a plan for a canal that would link the Altamaha River to the Turtle River, and thus by extension the Port of Brunswick. The Brunswick-Atlamaha Canal was a good idea when it started in 1836. But the project was plagued with financing and labor problems from start to finish. When it was finally completed 18 years later, the canal was already on the verge of obsolescence. By 1854, the railroad was coming into its own as a transporter of commerce and people.

The canal remains still today, a vegetation-clogged creek that flows but little as it bisects parts of the county and city. One of several historic markers for the canal can be found on the Golden Isles Parkway east of Canal Road, where its waters lap through a culvert beneath the roadway.

Brunswick did not really come into its own until after the Civil War, when a timber boom created an insatiable demand for Georgia pine. That pine also held turpentine and other resins known archaically as Naval stores. Brunswick would become a worldwide leader in providing Naval stores.

And that, folks, is a whole other story. That story would by necessity include the rise of the stately Oglethorpe Hotel, the devastating hurricane of 1898, the emergence of commercial shrimping, and Brunswick's contribution to the war effort as a shipbuilder during World War II.

Carr's place in early Brunswick history changes, but endures

A couple of historic markers bear his name in Brunswick's south end, but there is no Carr Street in the city, nor a Plug Point neighborhood in town.

It does not seem like too much to ask for the first European settler to make his stand in what would become Brunswick. Mark Carr, Captain of Boats for Gen. James Oglethorpe, was at least as remarkable as Sidney Lanier, though certainly not the *Marshes of Glynn* author's literary equal.

But c'mon, y'all. We all know that Carr settled in Brunswick's south end around 1740 on land granted him by Oglethorpe, a spread that would become known as the Plug Point tobacco plantation. Right? Well, kind of sort of.

It turns out we do not necessarily know what we know, or at least not all that we need to know about what we do know. And we should all get to know William Ruff, who just might be worthy of a Ruff Road running through Brunswick.

Aren't y'all glad we straightened all that out? Thanks to former City Manager Bill Weeks, I now have better understanding of the mainland's pre-Brunswick history and Carr's place in it. Weeks was city manager here from 2012-15, but the Brunswick resident is a lifelong archaeologist and anthropologist. He loves his chosen profession, which is evident from the research paper on Carr that Weeks recently shared with *The Brunswick News*.

His conclusion? According to Weeks, "there is no written evidence that Carr ever resided on the lower Brunswick peninsula." It turns out that nearby Blythe Island, just across the Turtle River from Brunswick, has more right to claim Carr as its own.

Just the same, there was a Plug Point in the south end of Brunswick, and it was linked closely to Carr. And the estate, also known as "Carrsfield," was once compared to the plantations of relatively civilized 18th Century Virginia, while the tobacco produced there was declared as fine as any produced in the young colonies.

Thanks to Weeks' research, we can now get to the bottom of this.

Born in 1702, Carr was the fifth son of an English nobleman. A military man, Carr was serving as quartermaster of a dragoons regiment in England when he decided in 1738 to throw in with Gen. Oglethorpe's new Georgia Colony. Carr obviously made a good impression on Oglethorpe after arriving at Fort Frederica on St. Simons Island.

In 1739, Oglethorpe granted Carr some 500 acres on Little Hermitage Island, nearly 10 miles north of present-day Brunswick on the Turtle River. Carr established a military outpost at the Hermitage settlement in the spring of 1740 to defend against Spanish and native threats.

A year later, Oglethorpe awarded Carr still more land — this being the 500 acres in the south end of Brunswick for which he is best known.

But if you want to get technical, the first plot in Brunswick was granted to Thomas Carr, then just 7 years old. Presumably, the property was granted in the name of Carr's son to get around red tape established by the Colony's trustees regarding multiple land grants.

Around this time, Oglethorpe made Carr the Captain of the Marine Company of Boats, which consisted of a pair of armed shallow-draft rowing galleys that were more accurately large dugout canoes carved from huge cypress trunks. On paper, the company was comprised of Capt. Carr, five lesser officers and 100 privates. But such numbers were hard to maintain on this outpost that served as first defense against the Spanish to the south.

While Carr was away on a recruiting trip in Virginia, natives attacked the military station at Hermitage. Four marines died in the attack, which left only the main house standing. The outpost was quickly rebuilt, fortified with four new blockhouses.

This historic marker in Brunswick recognizes Carr's contributions to early settlements here.

Then came July 7, 1742, when the decisive British victory at the Battle of Bloody Marsh on St. Simons Island effectively ended Spain's long-standing attempts to expand north of Florida. For his contribution to the battle's outcome, Carr earned yet one more piece of land, this time on Blythe Island.

In this less-vulnerable location, Carr established an estate consisting of two sturdy houses, several adjacent buildings and an expanse of cultivated fields. Carr still spent most of his time on Little Hermitage Island, which endured another native attack in March of 1744. Despite the attacks, a visitor remarked that Carr "keeps a very good house and lives much like a gentleman, has a good plantation ... "

About this same time, we learn that Carr's spread in present-day Brunswick is thriving under the supervision of one William Ruff. From the minutes of a Feb. 11, 1744 meeting of the Georgia trustees in England, one Plug Point visitor observed "that he has often seen Capt. Carr's plantation and never saw so fine a one in all Virginia; the William Ruff who lives at the said plantation produced last year a barrel of tobacco as good as any (in) Virginia ... "

After the military mustered out of Fort Frederica in 1749, and yet one more native attack on Hermitage, Carr ceded all claims in the Golden Isles and resettled on the Sunbury River below Savannah. However, he apparently could not stay away. Carr breathed his last breath at age 65 on Blythe Island.

"It is unclear how or when Carr returned to Blythe Island, where he died on December 7, 1767," Weeks wrote in his paper.

The exact location of the settlements that bear his name here in Glynn County remain elusive to archaeologists.

Wright Square: Digging up bones reveals city's tough start

Brunswick has been through many changes, struggles and transformations over the centuries, but all along a group of its early settlers have refused to go away.

Those persistent pioneers finally got our attention in 2014, but it is likely they still have plenty more to say to us.

Looking for a good local ghost story? Try Wright Square at Egmont and George streets on some moonlit night. There in the center of the green space is a monument to our nearly forgotten past. Etched in the base of the stone obelisk is this simple epithet: "Wright Square Burial Ground."

Long before the timeworn Oak Grove Cemetery was established as Brunswick's first recognized cemetery in 1839, the settlement's early homesteaders buried their dead beneath what is now Wright Square. Through its eras of progress and dormancy and regeneration, Brunswick's forward-looking inhabitants largely overlooked the resting place of many of our founders.

They tried to tell us. It was somewhat common knowledge way back when that a Revolutionary War veteran was buried around 1801 in an unmarked grave in front of the house of J. M. Burnett at 1103 Egmont St. That would be Benjamin Hart, who settled on 50 acres in Brunswick in 1796 with his more famous wife. Nancy Hart was the North Georgia backwoods woman who bamboozled a cadre of British soldiers, shooting one outright and holding four others captive for hanging.

But this old guard really got our attention around the turn of the century. While digging a new sewer trench along the northwest corner of Wright Square, city workers cut into the heart of past lives. The workers came across several human bones but kept on digging. Before the trench was complete, "a good-sized heap of

This monument was dedicated in 2014 to early Brunswick settlers who were buried below what is now Wright Square.

human bones were dug out," according to a report in the Brunswick Times-Advertiser.

The Times article noted that at least one tombstone remained in the area as far back as 1884, but that the mounds over the grave sites had long since leveled out and faded into obscurity.

In the early 20th Century, George Street was extended south across Wright Square, connecting Egmont and Carpenter streets. Those early settlers spoke up again several decades later, when the city decided to build a school on top of them in the section of Wright Square that now stood north of George Street.

When workers began laying the foundation for Glynn Middle School in 1953, you guessed it. More bones. Work was halted for a time. But city records held no written evidence that a burial ground ever existed there.

So students attended Glynn Middle there for decades, all the while the existence of a burial ground underneath persisting only as spooky rumors. The new Glynn Middle School facility opened in 2009 on Lanier Boulevard, leaving the building above the burial ground abandoned.

After trying for generations to get our attention, someone finally listened. That someone was Bill Weeks, then Brunswick's City Manager but previously a research associate with the South Carolina Institute for Archaeology and Anthropology. The old middle school was razed in 2012, which was the start of restoring Wright Square north of George Street as a city park.

Weeks, along with archaeologist Fred Cook and a crew of six hand-picked city public works employees, went digging at the site again. This project aimed to rediscover our past, not bury it.

"The excavations at Wright Square in the fall of 2012 were able to confirm the location of the earliest Brunswick city burial ground and establish with reasonable certainty the boundaries in each direction," Weeks concluded in his detailed 56-page report on the archaeological dig.

Weeks and his crew were able to identify 37 graves, dating from at least 1771 to 1840. Soil outlines, coffin nails, bones and other archaeological evidence helped identify the graves. Based on the overall size of this early graveyard, the team estimated between 65 and 75 early residents were buried there.

Bone fragments — a thigh bone, a shoulder bone, a jaw bone, a foot bone and a wisdom tooth — also indicate Brunswick's early residents were a "robust" and healthy bunch.

They had to be. Brunswick was a struggling outpost from the beginning, when Fort Frederica officer Mark Carr settled on Plug Point to grow tobacco in 1738. Carr sold his 1,000 acres to the British Crown in 1771. From there Brunswick staggered through a series of hopeful upstarts and disappointing setbacks before its emergence along with Georgia's post-Civil War timber boom.

Eight of the 37 graves belonged to children 5 or younger. This would suggest an infant mortality rate of 23 percent, much lower than average during this preindustrial era. But this likely indicates only that Brunswick was a tough place to raise kids back then, Weeks concluded. There were simply "fewer families and more numerous single or lone individuals," he noted.

A ceremony in April of 2014 honored these much-disturbed dead and dedicated the monument in their memory.

So, are they are still trying to get our attention? Who knows. Step out to Wright Square some moonlit night and find out for yourself.

Dart family tree branches out in Brunswick

The seed to one of Brunswick's most prolific family trees sprouted from Haddom, Conn., in 1764.

Cyrus Dart was but a boy when the Revolutionary War broke out 11 years later, but the patriotic young-ster managed to finagle a position as page to Gen. George Washington in the roughhewn Continental Army, so the story goes. But Cyrus' dad would have none of it, pulling the underage lad from service.

Undeterred, Cyrus later ran away to join up with the Army's 1st Connecticut Regiment, serving as a private in Capt. Stillwell's Company from 1782-83. Independence attained, Cyrus became a surgeon after the war and wandered south, eventually landing on St. Simons Island.

Branches of the Dart family tree have shaped and influenced events in Brunswick and the Golden Isles ever since. That includes the very founding of Brunswick, its churches and business community. A Dart was even on hand when the marshes of Glynn's splendor was famously put to rhyme and meter, good accounts have it. And a family member will most likely deliver a real zinger of a punchline at the next Brunswick Kiwanis Club meeting, if Bill Brown has anything to say about it. And the spry nonagenarian Dart (celebrating his 100th birthday on Dec. 3, 2019) descendant usually does have something to say about it.

You see, Cyrus begat Urbanus Dart, who begat William Robert Dart, who begat Ethel Grey Dart, who married William Hadley Brown and together they begat Bill Brown, now 98. Brown, a retired real estate agent, was born in the stately and once historic Dart House. The family home stood at 4 Glynn Ave. (U.S. Highway 17) for 137 years, from 1877 to right up until March of 2017.

Dart family descendant Bill Brown grew up in the ancestral home that once stood along U.S. Hwy. 17 near Gloucester Street. (Photo: Bobby Haven)

Bill Brown has two brothers and three sisters. And that is just one branch; at least three of Cyrus' eight children lived to produce offspring. Climbing through the thick foliage of the Dart's Glynn County lineage to encompass all the siblings, parents, cousins, nephews, nieces, uncles and aunts would require a lifetime membership to Ancestry.com.

So let's just go back to Cyrus. After completing his medical school training, Cyrus showed up on St. Simons Island in 1792, buying two lots in Old Town Frederica near the old fort. He married island native Ann Harris. Then he accepted a role in 1796 as a surgeon in the U.S. Army at Coleraine, a border settlement near Spanish Florida. Cyrus returned to the Golden Isles in 1802 to become quarantine officer for the Port of Brunswick.

It was in this capacity that Cyrus, his son Urbanus and a slave rowed out from St. Simons Island to meet a ship in need of a doctor on June 29, 1817. The boat capsized. Only Urbanus made it back to shore. Cyrus's body was never found. Urbanus and wife Ann lived until 1858. He is buried at Christ Church on St. Simons, where there also is a marker for Cyrus.

Urbanus Dart would lead a long and fulfilling life. Georgia's General Assembly granted Urbanus and William R. Davis the title to a large portion of Brunswick's undeveloped territory in 1826. Homes and businesses soon took root around a jail and a courthouse; Brunswick was incorporated as a municipality 10 years later.

Bill Brown said his great grandfather also granted lands for several of the city's churches, including St. Mark's Episcopal church and First African Baptist Church of Brunswick. "He wound up owning a substantial amount of the property in Brunswick," Brown recalls in the Stephen Doster's book, Georgia Witness: A Contemporary Oral History of the State. "He gave the land to most of the churches that were in Brunswick at that time."

Among Urbanus Dart's many offspring was Jacob E. Dart (1843-1917), who would go on to serve as mayor of Brunswick, as well as a member of the State Legislature. But one evening back in the 1870s, Jacob was strolling down Gloucester Street when the flute tunes floating from Friedlander Emporium caught his attention. Venturing inside he learned those sweet flute tunes were played by none other than Sidney Lanier, the poet. Both Confederate veterans of the still-fresh Civil War, the two men struck an immediate friendship.

Friendlander Emporium might have been a store, it might have been a saloon, and it likely was both, descendant Bill Brown said. Family lore holds that the two men bent their elbows over a few brews before strolling down to the waterfront to rest beneath an oak tree.

And that is where Lanier's muse turned its attention to the elusive beauty of the marshes of Glynn County, quite possibly influenced not just a little by their libations.

"They chatted and then walked ... and sat on the edge of the creek on a moonlit night with a spring tide," Brown recalls in Georgia Witness. "And Lanier got his inspiration to pen his poem ... My mother said he got his inspiration out of Friedlander's beer barrel."

It is believed the two rested at Lanier Oak, which folks today can visit at Overlook Park at the foot of Gloucester Street and U.S. 17.

Sidney Lanier: Man who famously put the marshes to rhyme was much more than just a poet

Shortly after arriving by happy accident in the Golden Isles nearly nine years ago, I found work at a grocery establishment in the Lanier Plaza.

The first time I attended a local cookout, we crossed the Sidney Lanier Bridge to get there. I often spent my lunch breaks back then at Marshes of Glynn Overlook Park, reading the plaques about this unique ecosystem and the man who extolled its virtues in rhyme and meter.

Then I would pass Lanier's Oak on my way back to work. I could go on — and on and on and on — but y'all get the point. You can't make three left turns and a lane change around here without running into something named for the poet and his lyrical homage to Glynn County's most recognizable attribute.

Soon after moving here I felt duty-bound to read "The Marshes of Glynn" — all 105 lines. "Glooms of the live-oaks, beautiful-braided and woven," his 1879 epic begins. The poem continues lovingly in this vein, waxing melodically about the "heavenly woods and glades ... wide sea-marshes ... woven shades of vine ... a league of marsh-grass waist high ... on the length and the breadth of the marvelous marshes of Glynn."

So Lanier is quite famous locally for this poem. But the term poet would hardly suffice to contain the experiences and pursuits that occupied Lanier's short life. In addition to poet, his profile includes soldier, scholar, prisoner of war, musician, composer, novelist, lawyer and critic.

For all his talent at describing the beauty in nature, Lanier's own life was marked with illness, poverty, and disillusionment. That life was nearing its end when Lanier penned "The Marshes of Glynn," while seeking a more hospitable climate for his tuberculosis.

The poet Sydney Lanier.

Lanier was born in Macon on Feb. 3, 1842. The son of a lawyer, he grew up with a love of reading and music that reinforced his appreciation of pastoral Southern traditions. He entered nearby Oglethorpe College at the tender age of 15 in 1857, graduating with honors three years later. The Civil War interrupted his plans of pursuing his education further. Following his loyalties to home, Lanier joined the Macon Volunteers and fought for the Confederacy.

Later in the war, Lanier had turned to piloting blockade runners. He was captured and sent to the Union prison at Point Lookout in Maryland, where he contracted the tuberculosis that would haunt him for the remainder of his years.

Looking back at his struggle, it is hard to believe some of us today call in sick with sniffles and a sore throat.

Lanier married Mary Day, and together they had four sons. Following the war, he returned to Macon, studied law and joined his father's practice. He rarely remained focused on one occupation for long. He taught school in Texas, Alabama and Georgia, often hovering desperately in poverty in between.

Lanier was passionate about music. Apparently, he was quite versed in the flute. He moved to Baltimore in 1873 and became the Peabody Orchestra's first flutist. During this time, he composed Danse des Moucherons (Midge Dance).

In 1867, Lanier wrote Tiger Lilies, a novel whose idealistic Southern protagonist struggles against the materialistic onslaught of changes wrought by the Civil War and Reconstruction. It was not a commercial success, but readers gave it high marks for the realistic battle scenes.

He lectured on Shakespeare at Johns Hopkins University, two volumes of which were published posthumously in 1902.

His love of music had obvious influence on his poetry. Like "The Marshes of Glynn," the poems "Corn" and "The Song of the Chattahoochee" are tributes to Georgia's natural beauty. These poems "reflect his accomplished infusion of music into poetic lines," according to one historian.

It was Lanier's fancy flute-work that first caught the attention of Jake Dart, a fellow Confederate veteran and member of a respected pioneering Brunswick family. Dart, a future Brunswick mayor, was walking past G. Friedlander Emporium near Gloucester and Newcastle streets when he heard a catchy melody.

"Passing by this store one night I heard a flute," Dart recalled years later. "Going in I saw Sidney Lanier, leaning against the counter. After a few minutes, he asked me to take a walk."

Dart family lore holds the Friedlanders also sold beer, at least a few of which Lanier and Dart shared before taking the walk. It is said the two new friends stopped to sit a spell under an oak beside the marsh, perhaps the same tree identified today as Lanier's Oak. "'How marvelous, how wonderfully beautiful the sinuous marshes of Glynn,'" Dart recalled Lanier saying.

Lanier and his family visited Brunswick off and on from the late 1860s into the 1870s, staying at the Albany Street home of his brother-in-law, Henry C. Day. Brunswick was yet another of several geographical cures Lanier sought for his affliction with tuberculosis.

Lanier's opus ode to our beautiful salt marsh was published in 1879. He died in 1881 in Lynn, N.C. He was just 39 years old.

However, Lanier's love for the impenetrable natural beauty of the salt marshes of Glynn County lives on.

Brunswick-Altamaha Canal misses the boat

Acres of empty home lots presently sit overgrown with weeds beneath the northern side of the Sidney Lanier Bridge, remnants of grand designs for the opulent Liberty Harbor community.

But this development project that collapsed along with the U.S. economy in 2008 ranks only second, at best, for promises of local prosperity that went unfulfilled.

Surely, the Brunswick-Altamaha Canal is the best thing that never happened to the Golden Isles. Pieces of the waterway remain still today, in the form of a vegetation-clogged ditch that runs 12 miles from a tributary of the Altamaha River in northern Glynn County to the Turtle River near the Port of Brunswick. Most prominently, this 164-year-old canal crosses beneath Golden Isles Parkway via a drainage culvert. Motorists whiz past the roadside historical marker there by the scores each day.

The canal was to unite the best of everything from Brunswick and Darien, combining each coastal community with what it lacked. But the enterprise was troubled from the start. Setbacks plagued the project for nearly 30 years, including wavering support, overreaching ambition, sweeping advances in transportation technology and the combined use of enslaved blacks and Irish immigrants in the labor force.

Darien sits at the mouth of the Altamaha River, which connected the city with inland trade in cotton and timber. Some 200 miles upstream, the Altamaha connects with the Ocmulgee and Oconee Rivers. The Ocmulgee provided navigation as far as Macon; the Oconee led to Milledgeville, which was the state capital back then.

But Darien had a lousy port, requiring skilled local knowledge to navigate cargo vessels through Doboy Sound and into the open

Atlantic. Still, based on its inland waterway connections, the Bank of Darien was a major financial institution in the mid-19th century.

On the other hand, Brunswick possessed an ideal, natural deep-water port. But Brunswick's port led to nowhere, its waters spilling with little economic value into the surrounding salt marsh. Yet the port's potential for oceangoing commerce had been recognized as early as 1789, when President George Washington named the Port of Brunswick one of five Ports of Entry to America. New York, Boston, Philadelphia and Baltimore were the others.

A canal was the obvious solution, connecting Darien's mighty artery to valuable inland commerce with Brunswick's deep-water port to the world. And a canal was especially appealing at the time. The opening of New York state's Erie Canal in 1825 showed America the most practicable way at the time to move raw goods from the interior to the coast.

"Georgians too witnessed the tremendous amount of trade and revenue generated by the Erie Canal and watched as New York City quickly became America's premier port and commercial city," historian Frank B. Gates wrote in the New Georgia En-

This stretch of the Brunswick-Altamaha Canal, cutting under Golden Isles Parkway, remains today.

cyclopedia.

Led by Retreat Plantation patriarch Thomas Butler King, a local contingent of planters and merchants received a state charter to build the Brunswick-Altamaha Canal in 1826. The project promptly went nowhere, languishing for another eight years.

The state legislature issued a new charter in 1834, again with King at the vanguard. As a Georgia state senator in the 1830s, King had connections in the capital. King recruited Loammi Baldwin Jr., a Harvard graduate and "the Father of Civil Engineering in America," to survey the canal route. It was to be 54 feet wide and 6 feet deep, with a 12-foot-wide towpath along the eastern bank.

Construction soon got under way with high hopes for the future. Seeing the economic value of connecting inland materials with an open port, the project began with financial backing from a group of Boston investors.

That northern money shriveled up after the Panic of 1837, a financial crisis that sunk the nation into a recession that would persist into the next decade. The project sputtered and stalled through the next 20 years.

By all accounts labor was an issue throughout. The brunt of the work originally was relegated to enslaved blacks from local plantations. Unskilled Irish immigrants were then brought in and finished the project. The plantation owners who backed the project preferred risking the lives of Irish immigrants in the hazardous labor of canal construction. It was strictly business.

"No doubt some planters believed it was more economic to use Irish laborers who had no intrinsic value as property for the sometimes-dangerous work on the canal rather risk their own slaves," wrote Timothy James Lockey in his book, *Lines in the Sand: Race and Class in Lowcountry Georgia, 1750-1860.*

The canal finally opened in June of 1854, according to one Savannah newspaper. By then, however, canals were fading from relevance. Railroads were making tracks across the nation, emerging as the fastest and most efficient means known to humankind for transporting goods and folks.

"Just how much the canal was used is a matter of question," concluded the American Canal Society.

Opulent Oglethorpe Hotel once stood as crowning Jewel of downtown Brunswick

For a local perspective on the perpetually-restless American spirit, look no further than the vacant lot at the entrance to downtown Brunswick.

Chances are you've driven past it dozens of times, scarcely taking notice of the site that once housed a burgeoning monument to good taste and refinement. Yes, at one time the majestic Oglethorpe Hotel occupied that patch of dirt, grass and weeds at the juncture where U.S. Highway 341 splits into Newcastle and Bay streets at the entrance to downtown Brunswick.

For 70 years the Oglethorpe presided over the city's downtown district, three stories high with 267 palatial feet of frontage commanding a view of the East River. Conical towers rose on the horizon of its genteel gothic architecture, which also featured a marble tiled rotunda and a circular balcony overlooking a courtyard fountain amid lush gardens and landscaping.

Then, in 1958, its owners tore the Oglethorpe down. In its place rose a boxy Holiday Inn, identical to the thousands of Holiday Inns that were then sprouting across America. The rest of the former Oglethorpe site gave way to a J.C. Penney store.

That Holiday Inn eventually would suffer the same fate as the Oglethorpe. However, the building that once housed the J.C. Penney franchise still stands, serving today as a provisioner of, perhaps fittingly, antiques.

And that vacant lot — commonly referred to as the "Oglethorpe block" — is now a revolving source of hope for better days to come in Brunswick. City and county elected officials have hemmed and hawed over its future for years, poring over such options as a convention center or yet another hotel, or both.

The Oglethorpe Hotel.

There was a time when this site represented the best of what Brunswick had to offer.

Designed by noted architect J.A. Wood of Poughkeepsie, N.Y., the Oglethorpe Hotel was once considered among the largest hotels in the South. This was in keeping with the great expectations surrounding Brunswick during the economic boom experienced here at the end of the 19th Century. After nearly 100 years of bad timing and war-torn setbacks since its founding in 1771, Brunswick finally came into its own as a port city in the decades following the Civil War.

Tall Georgia pine fueled this economic engine. Brunswick emerged as a hub for shipping timber to a westward expanding nation. It also became a global leader in the provision of Naval stores such as turpentine and varnish. City docks were stacked with barrels and barrels of naval stores, often bound for Europe and beyond on huge oceangoing vessels.

The pine was felled in central Georgia, lashed together in huge square rafts and floated down the Altamaha River to the coast at

Darien. From there, pine was ferried at high tide to Brunswick and St. Simons Island through a natural water artery known as 3-mile Cut.

"The ports of Brunswick and St. Simons became the worldwide leader of shipping naval stores," said Buddy Sullivan, a noted Coastal Georgia historian and author of more than 25 books on the subject. "Thousands of barrels of turpentine would line the docks to be shipped around the world."

Railroads such as the Brunswick and Western and the Georgia Coastal further strengthened Brunswick's overland connections to the outside world. At the start of the Civil War in 1861, Brunswick's population stood at a modest 1,000 folks. With that brutal war behind them and the bounty of Georgia pines ahead of them, Brunswick had blossomed into a thriving city of 9,000 folks by 1870.

The boom times peaked in 1900, when a record 112 million board feet of Georgia pine was timbered. Poor stewardship caused this natural resource to taper off after the turn of the 20th Century, but the regal Oglethorpe Hotel carried on in downtown Brunswick.

It survived the devastating 1898 hurricane that struck Brunswick head on, and it persevered through the Great Depression that followed the 1929 stock market crash. The Oglethorpe was still there when Brunswick emerged as a major contributor on the home front during World War II, when a shipyard on the Brunswick River produced 99 Liberty Ships toward the war effort.

Native son Bill Brown, now 100, remembers the Oglethorpe hosting a dinner to honor the first Brunswick Pulp and Paper worker to head off to war. "Oh, hell yeah," said Brown. "It was just a grand hotel."

A Darien native, Sullivan recalls accompanying family in his boyhood on day trips to the Oglethorpe for fancy Sunday dining.

"I have fond memories of going to the Oglethorpe to have dinner after church," Sullivan said. "But it was torn down and sold for scrap. They put up one of those antiseptic Holiday Inns."

Call to Worship has deep roots in downtown Brunswick

B ack when I was living in Brunswick a few years ago, a short noontime bicycle ride down Newcastle Street one sunny day placed me virtually all alone in the heart of the city's commercial district.

Vacant diagonal parking spaces lined both sides of "Main Street," behind which every establishment was closed except for a pub and a restaurant that barely served half a dozen customers between them. Far from being deserted, however, Brunswick was actually bustling with folks on this day.

A couple blocks over, parking lots overflowed, and cars lined long stretches of Union and Reynolds streets. Ditto for the areas of Gloucester and Egmont streets, Norwich and Monk streets, and elsewhere throughout the city. Pedaling around town, playing hooky from my own church, I felt a serene sense of continuity on this typical Sunday in the South.

For all the stately homes in Historic Downtown Brunswick, few architectural gems shine brighter than the city's many venerable old churches. Keeping the Sabbath has long been a revered tradition in Brunswick, dating back at least to 1838.

That is when a congregation of Methodists established themselves in the young city. We know this congregation today as Brunswick First United Methodist Church, 1400 Norwich St. In the beginning, Brunswick's early Methodists were part of a preaching circuit of the Florida Conference of the Methodist Episcopal Church and had no permanent house of worship. They met at several locations, including the Glynn Academy schoolhouse.

The first church built at United Methodist's present site arose in 1861. Bad timing. The Civil War broke out that year, and Brunswick's residents abandoned the city to occupying Yankee troops a year later. Services did not resume there until war's end in 1865. By the turn of the century, that original church gave way to the current structure. The first sermon delivered inside that sanctuary occurred on Dec. 20, 1904.

As early as 1844, Catholic Mass was being celebrated in the Brunswick home of the Jekyll Island duBignons on Union Street. The first Catholic chapel was erected in 1868 at Egmont and Mansfield streets on land donated by Urbanus Dart. Dart, a former city mayor and member of a founding Brunswick family, donated much of the land on which early churches were built. In 1884, St. Frances Xavier Catholic Church was dedicated at its present site on Hanover Square in downtown Brunswick.

Beginning in 1858, the original congregation of St. Mark's Episcopal Church also made use of the Glynn Academy schoolhouse, as would several other ascending churches in their early years. (Established in 1788, Glynn Academy is the second oldest public school in Georgia; the building in question was constructed in 1840.)

Regrouping after the Civil War, St. Mark's claimed 98 members in 1868. Six years later, the first wooden structure went up on the site of the present St. Mark's Church at 900 Gloucester St. A bell tower was added in the 1890s and the existing structure was fortified in 1911 with the "cement bricks" that stand today. The Rev. Henry Lucas led the congregation from 1876 up until his death in 1900, after which he was laid to rest beneath the altar in an unmarked grave.

Worshippers now gather by the hundreds each Sunday at First Baptist Church at 708 Mansfield St., but the church's inception began humbly in November of 1855. The first Baptists to gather in Brunswick did so in — you guessed it — the Glynn Academy schoolhouse. The congregation included nine white members and 70 blacks. It was led by the Rev. T.B. Cooper.

The original Baptist church building was constructed in 1858 at H and Union streets, with full immersion baptisms taking place in a nearby saltwater creek. Construction of the present church at Mansfield and Union streets began in 1887 and was completed three years later.

First United Methodist Church, among the oldest in Brunswick.

A congregation of 200 assumed a $35,000 debt to see that church become a reality.

Just down the street from First Baptist, another large church stands at the corner of Union and George streets. First Presbyterian Church took root in 1867, shortly after the Civil War's end. Its charter members included two black residents. The first church building at 1105 Union St. was dedicated on Dec. 18, 1873.

Founded by St. Mark's, St. Athanasius Episcopal Church opened to serve the black community in Brunswick in 1885. The tabby revival-style building was completed around 1890 at 1321 Albany St. and stands today as "one of the best examples of a historic tabby structure that is still being used as originally intended by the designers," preservationist Taylor Davis has noted.

The congregants of First African Baptist Church of Brunswick first met beneath an oak grove between Gloucester and F streets some 155 years ago, during the Civil War. The congregation built its tongue-and-groove wood church at 1416 Amherst St. in 1867 on land donated by Urbanus Dart. With some modifications, that structure of understated elegance still serves a predominantly black Brunswick congregation to this day.

So, Newcastle's business district might look fairly dead come Sunday. But the spirit will be very much alive elsewhere in Brunswick, as folks answer that time-honored call to worship at long-established churches throughout the city.

Temple's tale that of the American Dream

At the corner of Egmont and Monck streets in Historic Brunswick there rises a genteel and dignified house of prayer. The structure complements nicely its immediate spiritual neighbors, St. Mark's Episcopal and First United Methodist churches.

For nearly 128 years, this venerable old building has stood as testimony to its worshippers' devotion to their faith and of their commitment to this community as a whole. It was founded in 1890 as the heart of Brunswick's rising Jewish community, but Temple Beth Tefilloh also came to represent that community's faith in the American Dream.

The Moorish Revival-style synagogue features an onion-dome tower, typical of this architectural form. But that temple dome is flanked on the entrance's other side by a squared gothic tower, more in keeping with the many Christian churches in the neighborhood.

The dark hardwood pine of the ceilings, the support columns and the pews inside this synagogue cast a soothing, reverential tone. The beautifully ornate keyhole-frame stained-glass windows are originals, installed when the synagogue's initial congregation of 22-families were joined by many of their Christian neighbors to joyfully dedicate its opening on Nov. 7, 1890.

Never mind if the soft white walls inside this building could talk. Every inch of this synagogue tells a story. It is a classically American tale, one of sturdy immigrant stock arriving on these shores, not looking back, and embracing this country's promises of freedom.

In fact, sleepy little Brunswick just might be as good a place as any to document the history of the Jewish experience in America. (For that matter, some of the first Jews in the New World landed in Savannah, contributing significantly to the success of Gen. James Oglethorpe's Georgia Colony in the 1730s.) While a

Temple Beth Tefilloh. (Photo: Bobby Haven)

scattering of Jewish families already lived in Brunswick, those who would establish Temple Beth Tefilloh began arriving in the 1870s. These families had immigrated from Germany and neighboring central European communities. They established homes in Brunswick just as the late 19th Century timber boom rejuvenated the local economy following the ravages of the Civil War.

Led by Jewish immigrant David Glauber, Brunswick's Temple Beth Tefilloh congregation was officially established in 1886. That is the same year the Statue of Liberty arose in another harbor city up north, beckoning to our shores the world's "huddled masses yearning to breathe free."

This energetic group in Brunswick caught on quickly. They assimilated into the larger community, joining the local professional, merchant and municipal ranks. But these diligent newcomers also were determined to build a permanent house of prayer, which is the literal Hebrew translation of Temple Beth Tefilloh.

The structure was designed by none other than Alfred Eichberg, himself a Jew who also was one of the South's most recognized architects. Eichberg also designed Brunswick's Old City Hall and many of the larger homes in Historic Brunswick.

The building we see today at 1326 Egmont St. is basically the same structure that came to fruition for the congregation in just a few short years.

"They were incredibly industrious, because four years later they built this," said Mason Stewart, a Brunswick native and resident historian of Temple Beth Tefilloh.

And the synagogue's opening was a big deal, both locally and for the Jewish American community at large. The local newspaper of the day described the dedication as one of the social events of the year, Stewart said. Likewise, Jewish dignitaries from across the nation were on hand, including Rabbi Isaac Meyer Wise, founder of the American Reform Judaism movement.

It is important to note that the founders of our local Jewish community were members of Reform Judaism. The reform movement arose out of traditional Orthodox Judaism in the 19th Century, permitting its followers to assimilate more freely within the secular world.

Rabbi Wise's American Reform movement put a stars-and-stripes patriotic twist on this new direction for Judaism. He encouraged Jewish people to proudly proclaim themselves Americans, who just happened to practice their freedom of worship in temples.

As Meyer himself said at the dedication, "for our own part, we are Jews in the synagogue and Americans elsewhere."

The folks at Temple Beth Tefilloh took this to heart. At the time of the dedication, temple members included the chief of the fire commission, the city treasurer, the city recorder and several representatives on Brunswick's Board of Trade.

It has been that way all along. By the 1960s, members of the local Jewish community were taking leadership roles in civic organizations such as the Rotary, Elk's and Brunswick Women's clubs.

Temple Beth Tefilloh's American success story continues today under the leadership of Rabbi Rachael Bregman. The temple's first female rabbi, Bregman is the contemporary epitome of everything those early founders envisioned. Smart, witty, wise and compassionate, Bregman also is well-versed in the stories this temple has to tell.

"Even picking a Moorish Revival style here speaks to a desire for the (Jewish) community to be integrated in with everyone else," Bregman said. "It was pretty new (to Judaism) even in the late 1800s that you could consider being American first and Jewish second. They just wanted to be a part of the rest of the community."

Port of Brunswick served valuable role in the cause of liberty during World War II

From atop the towering Sidney Lanier Bridge, the view of the Brunswick River's northern shore offers an unadorned tribute to this community's commitment to America's veterans.

A row of aging maritime slips cuts into the shoreline, a reminder of the time when the Golden Isles' citizenry galvanized itself almost single-mindedly to the task of winning World War II. From 1943 to 1945, some 85 newly-built Liberty Ships were launched on these slipways, destined to haul supplies and armaments to the war effort in the European and Pacific theaters.

As vital as these cargo ships were to the war effort, so too were the folks who built them. The local population exploded during the war years, from less than 15,000 to nearly 65,000. The shipyard run by the J.A. Jones Co. alone employed 16,000 people — men who were too old or otherwise ineligible for military service, along with women whose competence with heavy equipment helped forge the national identity of Rosie the Riveter.

"The population of Brunswick just exploded over the war years with workers coming in to work on the Liberty Ships," said Buddy Sullivan, a noted Coastal Georgia historian and author. "You can see how valuable this area was to the overall war effort."

With its established deep-water port, Brunswick was a natural choice when the U.S. government began scouting the nation's coastlines for sites to establish shipbuilding yards. Brunswick's was one of 17 shipyards that cropped up along the nation's coastlines. From South Portland, Maine, to Mobile, Ala., to Portland, Ore., these yards churned out more than 2,700 Liberty Ships.

Rex Thompson and Brunswick Marine secured the original contract. It called for a shipyard with six slipways, allowing con-

Remnants of the slipways where newly-built Liberty Ships launched into the Brunswick River can still be seen today.

struction of half a dozen ships simultaneously. This shipbuilding concern established the infrastructure along the Brunswick River and began work on its first Liberty Ship in early 1942. But the government canceled the contract, raising concerns about the pace of production.

J.A. Jones, which also operated a Liberty Ship yard in Panama City, Fla., won the new contract and took over the shipyard. Brunswick Marine remained in the game, however, building coastline fuel and transport ships, as well as the bow sections of amphibious landing craft, according to the book, *Brunswick: A Book of Memories*.

Brunswick and environs, meanwhile, swelled at a dizzying pace. With help from federal and state government agencies, about 7,200 new dwellings materialized in Glynn County virtually overnight. "Temporary housing facilities arose on every available lot," according to *Book of Memories*. "Some brick apartments, some wooden ones, covered the landscape throughout the city."

The Jones company often had to ship in food and other supplies to meet the needs of its stalwart workforce. And they were all that. In 1944, the shipyard earned the Maritime Commission "M" for outstanding achievement and also was awarded the Gold Eagle in March when it bested all yards on the eastern seaboard in ship deliveries in 1944.

Brunswick's commitment to the troops truly shined in late 1944, when the government challenged all shipyards with six slipways to produce as many Liberty Ships by year's end.

The folks at Brunswick's shipyardmanaged to exceed that challenge, launching seven before 1945 dawned. With American troops reeling from the German onslaught during the Battle of the Bulge that raged that December, more than 2,000 Brunswick shipbuilding workers were on the job Christmas Day. They also gave their holiday overtime pay for that shift to the war effort, which totaled about $16,000.

While invaluable to the war's successful conclusion, Liberty Ships were not much to look at from the standpoint of nautical aesthetics. "A dreadful looking object," is how President Roosevelt described them. Time Magazine dubbed the Liberty Ship the "Ugly Duckling." And the ships were not without problems, including a brittle makeup and a tendency toward cracks in hulls and decks.

But the Liberty Ships were efficient. The steel ships were 447 feet long with a cargo capacity of about 10,000 tons. The 2,500 horsepower steam engines provided a maximum speed of a trudging 11 knots.

The ships typically crossed in convoys under Naval escort. But trepidation accompanied the ships' Atlantic crossings, as German U-boats prowled the seas. Of the ships constructed at Brunswick, one was sunk by a torpedo in the Mediterranean and three others were sunk by mines.

But those German U-boats just could not keep track of all the Liberty Ships churned out by the American workforce, Sullivan notes. While our soldiers, marines and sailors outfought the enemy, the support they received back home in places like Brunswick helped seal the victory.

"Americans were building Liberty Ships three or four times faster than the Germans could possibly hope to sink them," Sullivan said. "So the Germans eventually realized they were losing the war on Liberty Ships. This gives you an idea of what a great asset this shipbuilding operation was to the war."

Nothing nostalgic about 1915's mass shooting in Brunswick

On the peaceful morning of March 6, 1915, downtown Brunswick looked as if it were posing for a Norman Rockwell painting of Americana at leisure.

Then Monroe Phillips walked into the second-floor office of the Hon. Harry F. Dunwoody with a loaded double-barrel shotgun — blasting away and killing the judge and seriously wounding a colleague.

Calmly, Phillips walked back downstairs, reloading as he went, before stepping out into that picturesque downtown morning calm to unleash carnage and death.

The Brunswick News deftly captured the diametrical extremes of that morning in the opening sentence of an article chronicling the mass shooting for the next day's paper.

"Within the twinkling of an eye, in a community full of peace and happiness, under skies as beautifully blue as those which hung above the homes of our first ancestors, Brunswick's hospital was pressed into service yesterday morning, while Brunswick's undertaking establishments were converted into veritable morgues," The News reported.

In a horrifying span of 10 minutes, a man with a grudge and a gun turned downtown Brunswick into a bloody shooting gallery, killing five and wounding 32.

"On he went like some crazed demon, shooting as he advanced with the wide world for his target, caring little who he murdered or why," *The News* reported.

It ended only when two hometown heroes armed themselves and gunned the deranged Phillips down inside a local drug store as the 61-year-old was reloading for still more bloodshed.

"In the meantime the avenging spirit was busy, but the man

who had inflicted death so calmly was doomed to meet that article by the same instrument in which he was dispensing it," noted *The News*.

It would be superficial to attempt at this point a comparison with Phillips' bloody rampage and the soul-numbingly commonplace mass shootings of 21st century America. Advanced firearms technology and contemporary mental illness debates aside, suffice it to say that such senseless slaughter of random innocents is nothing new. The symptoms, methods and similarities are inescapable.

Monroe Phillips was a surly man on his best days, openly susceptible to slights real or imagined, personal or professional. He was slow to make friends, quick to take offense. He moved to Brunswick around 1909 from Bibb County, arriving on sound financial footing from his dealings in the timber and real estate business. He and wife Ophelia had three children.

He was something of a land speculator in Brunswick, "a sort of financial plunger, real estate operator and more or less business man," *The News* reported. But Phillips' fortunes were on the decline in his final years. He spread blame and lawsuits all over town. Prominent among these was the litigious contention that respected businessman Albert Fendig shorted him $25,000 in a real estate deal.

In the end, however, a dispute over $75 and a shipping barge sale was the last straw. That was the down payment on a barge he sold, but the deal was held up by several Savannah creditors. A phone call between Judge Dunwoody and Phillips' wife that morning concerning the matter did not go well, or it was at least misinterpreted.

When his wife reported the conversation to Phillips, the big man grabbed his shotgun and stormed over to what is still known today as the Dunwoody Building, at Newcastle and Gloucester streets. Standing over 6 feet and weighing more than 200 pounds, he brushed past Dunwoody's secretary and barged into Dunwoody's office. Without fanfare, he shot Dunwoody in the head, killing him. Also in the office was real estate businessman Albert M. Way, who failed to escape the blast from the second barrel, taking a hit to the face. Way survived, but he lost an eye.

Former Brunswick policeman L.C. Padgett and attorney Eustace C. Butts rushed to the building just as Phillips had reloaded. He shot Padgett fatally at the foot of the stairs, wounding Butts in the leg with the same salvo. He walked to the nearby office of Albert Fendig, causing panic in a busy women's boutique along the way with an otherwise harmless blast through a front window. As fate would have it, Fendig was not in. W.K. Boston, perhaps Phillips' only friend in town, was in at Fendig's office. "I am not going to kill you; you have been my friend," Phillips told Boston.

The dying Padgett had been taken to Branch's Drug Store and Phillips headed there next. He shot and killed streetcar conductor George W. Asbell as he exited Branch's. Phillips next mortally wounded 20-year-old Gunnar Tolnas, knocking him off his bicycle in the street. Ernest McDonald was fatally wounded as he stepped out of a barber shop.

During the mayhem, Butts had hobbled into United Supply Company and procured a shotgun and shells. R. J. Minehan picked up a .32 caliber pistol from the store at the same time.

Police officer Rex Deaver, 23 and just two months on the force, exchanged gunfire with Phillips through the front door of Branch's. Deaver's service weapon was no match for the "10-bore Parker shotgun" and young Deaver died in the line of duty.

As that exchange unfolded, the now-armed Butts and Minehan attacked from a side door of Branch's. A fusillade from Minehan's handgun struck Phillips at least once, but Butts' shotgun dealt the fatal blows that ended the nightmare on Newcastle Street.

"Phillips was reloading for another shot when Butts fired," *The News* reported. "Phillips sank to the floor shot through the kidneys. He lived a few minutes."

Portuguese fishermen helped launch Georgia's shrimp industry

Wild Georgia Shrimp had it pretty good around here until the likes of John Martin and Joe Santos arrived on our shores following World War I.

These two men were among the early wave of Portuguese refugees who crossed the Atlantic Ocean early in the 20th Century, only to chart a course right back into the sea to reap its bounty. Suddenly, our local shrimp began showing up in large numbers on menus and dinner tables from here to New York City.

By the 1930s, the public's newfound taste for these crustaceans had filled the docks along Brunswick's East River with shrimp boats, all of them captained and crewed by stout-hearted Old-World mariners. Those vessels would include the seven trawlers Joe Santos and partner John Mendes owned jointly in the Union Shrimp Company. John Martin captained his own shrimp boat out of Brunswick, the Miss Martin. Manuel Rocha and his boat the Liberty also were there.

Afternoons and evenings were festive family affairs down in the south end of Brunswick back then, recalls Mary Theresa Martin. Families would gather in Hanover Square and Queens Square, with children playing and mothers preparing picnic dinners. Men like Mary Theresa's Dad, John Martin, and her Uncle Joe Santos would occupy the park benches, or those in front of Old City Hall. There they would shoot the bull about the day's catch, and the haul that awaited their nets the following morning.

"My Mamma used to say they caught more shrimp on those benches than out in the ocean," said Mary Theresa, who is now 88 and still living in Brunswick's south end. "If those trees could

Joe Santos and John Mendes started Union Shrimp Co., a shrimp fishing operation that was part of the first Blessing of the Fleet in Brunswick.

talk, they would all speak Portuguese. That's all you heard down there. Hanover was like the hangout."

Some folks, Mary Theresa among them, will tell you that these Portuguese immigrants created both supply and demand for shrimp in America. While that is not entirely accurate, these enterprising new arrivals certainly played a major role in transforming a menial occupation into a national industry.

Chalk it up to good timing. And family tradition.

Portugal is a small nation awash in salt air just above where the Atlantic Ocean meets the warm waters of the Mediterranean Sea. These men came here from a long line of fisherman who were adept at wresting a living from wild, open waters. Over there, this meant setting out into the Atlantic Ocean in small dories from larger ships to catch cod with hand lines. (Think Spencer Tracy's endearing Portuguese character in the movie "Captains Courageous.")

The Portuguese who settled in Brunswick came first though Ellis Island in New York, beginning with the end of WWI in 1918. Mary Theresa's mom (also Mary Theresa) was just 10 years old when she made the crossing with her brother, Joe Santos, himself just a teenager. They crossed in the steerage of a ship carrying American troops home from the war, Mary Theresa said.

But the other side of Ellis Island left them shivering in the frigid northern climes. "They didn't like it up north," she said. "It was too cold."

The early migration path from Ellis Island led these post-war Portuguese immigrants first to nearby Fernandina Beach, Fla. That is where modern shrimping really dawned, beginning in 1913 when Massachusetts transplant Billy Corkum invented the otter trawl net. The otter trawl features weighted wooden doors which open wide under throttle and drag along the bottom, greatly increasing the catch.

Also, air conditioning and ice machines had come along early in the 20th Century, making it possible to ship our local delicacy fresh to points north. (Brunswick's David Davis Co. started in 1915, shipping boiled shrimp canned in brine as far away as Canada and England.)

But soon Fernandina Beach could not hold them all, and folks like Joe Santos were eager to test new waters. He and many other Portuguese immigrants would find a welcome port in Brunswick. Among them was John Martin, who later met and married a grownup Mary Theresa Santos in Brunswick. The daughter named for her mom was born in 1929.

Years later, Mary Theresa's Uncle Joe and his business partner were honored by the Georgia State Chamber of Commerce, testament to the impact of these industrious immigrants. The "Accolade of Appreciation" thanked the "Union Shrimp Company for economic contributions, high standards of citizenship, and participation in Georgia's progress since 1931."

Indeed, America's coastal shrimping industry that now stretches from Wilmington, N.C., to Corpus Christi, Texas, in the Gulf of Mexico owes a debt of gratitude to Brunswick's Portuguese immigrants.

"They really started a whole new industry that wasn't there before they came," Mary Theresa said.

Another Portuguese contribution to American shrimping is the annual blessing of the fleet, a tradition that takes place each spring in coastal hamlets throughout the South. The very first

Blessing of the Fleet likely took place right here on the East River, says Manny Rocha, 78. It occurred in 1938, shortly after shrimper Manuel Boa had returned from a pilgrimage to his homeland.

Boa brought back a statue of Our Lady of Fatima, which to this day resides at St. Francis Xavier Catholic Church in Brunswick across the street from Hanover Square. As they have for the several generations now, each Mother's Day members of the Knights of Columbus at St. Francis Xavier take the Brazilian wood statue on a promenade through Hanover Square and back into the church.

This faithful procession would be immediately recognizable to Manual Rocha Sr., the Portuguese fisherman who came to America so long ago for a better life.

"My father would leave out of here at three in the morning, every day," said Manny, a retired AT&T technician. "Rain or shine, hot or cold, that boat had to go."

Hollywood comes calling in Golden Isles

I like old movies, a category that has expanded, quite alarmingly, to include flicks that were filmed in my lifetime.

Fay Wray's beauty contrasted King Kong's beastly mitt but little onscreen when I first developed my love for old movies, just as Humphrey Bogart and Ingrid Bergman's star-crossed love in Casablanca unfolded only in shades of black and white. But, heck, a couple of months ago the Turner Classic Movies channel showed me a colorful film that hit theaters when I was a seventh-grader.

However, it was not the era so much as the place that drew my attention that night to this movie, *Conrack*. The elusive blueish-brown hues of the brackish creeks that wound through golden-green salt marsh grasses on my television screen immediately struck a familiar chord. Likewise, the oceanfront beaches and distinctly-Southern Victorian homes were comfortingly recognizable.

Then, a couple of nights ago, I was thumbing through *"Brunswick: A Book of Memories,"* when the reason for this film's familiarity smacked me broadside. *Conrack* was filmed right here in the Golden Isles in 1973. St. Simons Island served as the backdrop for sheltered Daufuskie Island, S.C., while Brunswick stood in for Beaufort, S.C.

Based on a biographical Pat Conroy book, *Conrack* tells a charming story about a hippie teacher who returns to his Low Country Carolina roots in 1969. The Gullah children he teaches are innocently isolated from 20th Century America on a barrier island. It is a pretty good movie, starring Jon Voigt, an Academy Award-winning actor from back in the day.

The *Conrack* film crew's visit nearly 45 years ago was not the first time Hollywood came calling in Glynn County. Most of us can scarcely forget that it has only been a couple of years since movie star Ben Affleck took over downtown Brunswick to film *Live By Night*.

But Brunswick's movie credits go all the way back to 1955.

That is when Brunswick and the stately old Oglethorpe Hotel stood in as the backdrop for *The View from Pompey's Head*. Parts of the Twentieth Century Fox film also were shot on Jekyll Island.

The movie was based on writer Hamilton Basso's best-selling novel of the same name. It is the story of a New York lawyer who returns to his native coastal Carolina town, which he left in the first place in disillusion over the community's unresolved racial and class strife. He returns to help restore royalties owed an aging Southern writer and mentor, tangling romantically in the process with an old flame now married to a boorish businessman. The whole thing unfolds in black and white, with men in sensible suits and ladies in flowing dresses, just as old movies should be.

Brunswick beat out more than two dozen Southern cities that were courting the filmmakers, according to a 1955 article in The Brunswick News. Brunswick leaders even put together a book highlighting the city's virtues, which then Mayor Millard Copeland sent to Philip Dunne, the film's director.

"Though about 30 towns answered the studio's specifications for the type of scenery, streets and buildings ... it was the Brunswick Chamber of Commerce (Ruby Berrie) who prepared a huge book proving Brunswick had not some but all that the film needed," The News reported.

Scenes filmed at the Oglethorpe Hotel created quite a stir among the locals, Mary McGarvey recalled in Brunswick: A Book of Memories. It would be but one more bittersweet memory of the Oglethorpe, which was destroyed in the 1960s to make way for a Holiday Inn.

"There was much local excitement when time arrived to film the scenes at the Oglethorpe Hotel," McGarvey wrote. "It was our crown jewel. Little did we know that the ball of demolition was figuratively hanging over it."

Jon Voigt and local children in Conrack, filmed in the Golden Isles.

And the movie? It was OK. Reviewer Leonard Maltin gave it 2 1/2 out of 4 stars on TCM's webpage (www.tcm.com). The book, which hovered on the best-selling list for 40 weeks in 1954, is certainly better.

Ditto for *Conrack*, or any movies based on the sterling words of Pat Conroy. Still, TCM's overall review of Conrack gives it 4 out of 5 stars. Voigt actually plays Conroy in this movie based on the writer's memoir, *The Water is Wide*. The movie's title comes from the children's mispronunciation of the author's name.

Many of Conrack's younger stars likely walk among us today. Director Martin Ritt recruited local black children to star as the students in Voigt's island classroom. Ritt apparently chose well, according to a New York Times reviewer at the time.

"And (Voigt) deserves special credit for acting with the 21 children selected from a local school — who could snatch a scene from many a seasoned veteran," wrote Nora Sayre.

Another local shining through in the movie was the McKinnon House in Brunswick's Historic Old Town. The Victorian home built in 1902 serves as a backdrop for a climactic moment when Conrack and the island kids visit the school superintendent's home during their first time trick-or-treating in Beaufort.

"The owners (of the McKinnon House) in 1972 were Nelson and Hazel Westbrooks, who recall showing Jon Voigt around the house that they had purchased just two weeks before," according to A Book of Memories.

Local civil rights struggle was Quiet Conflict

I t is a hearty chuckle, tinged with a wistful tone of nostalgia, maybe even a hint of longing for the old days.

"He was a thorn," says Robert Griffin, 81, pointing to the man filling the broad flat screen on the television.

In grainy black and white from 1964, a local leader of the White Citizen's Council is droning on about his group's opposition to desegregating the Golden Isles. Moments later, the CBS documentary crew is talking to a white Brunswick restaurant owner who was elected to office on a decidedly segregated ticket.

"He met me at the door with a baseball bat when I tried to go into his restaurant," Griffin said, chuckling again and shaking his head.

Sitting in the living room of Griffin's sturdy old house off G Street, I am honored to visit with one of the men who helped us get from there to here. Born in 1961, I am barely old enough to remember those days when the South appeared in sharp contrasts of black and white. Fortunately, succeeding generations have no first-hand knowledge of a segregated South.

Folks like Griffin can never forget. He once took a slap in the face at a "Whites Only" lunch counter in Nashville — retribution for participating in one of Dr. King's sit-ins while attending Tennessee State University.

By the time Griffin arrived in Brunswick to teach band at blacks-only Risley High, he did not flinch at racist restaurant owners or White Citizens Council chiefs. Neither did the Rev. J.C. Hope, pastor at Zion Baptist Church and leader of the community's newly-formed NAACP chapter. There were others, Griffin said — Geneva Lyde, George Miller, Issodora Hunter, Venus Holmes ... too many black leaders, in fact, to mention without unintentionally passing over so many more who are deserving of note.

But Griffin is quick to point out that this community's desegre-

Local Civil Right leader Robert Griffin.
(Photo: Bobby Haven)

gation efforts were by no means a one-sided affair. Racist agitators such as those mentioned above were in the minority among white community leaders in the Golden Isles, Griffin said.

"That was the secret of our whole success here," says Griffin, a local NAACP coordinator in those days. "We had reasonable people to work with. This is why we were able to move forward."

And that brings us to this old CBS documentary that Griffin is sharing with me. It is titled, "Brunswick, Georgia: Quiet Conflict." Conflicting quietly was apparently a positive thing back then. While things came to blows between blacks and whites in Savannah above us, Jacksonville below us, and elsewhere throughout the Deep South during the Civil Rights struggle, Brunswick was a comparative model of decorum and diplomacy.

So much so that the Columbia Broadcasting System sent a film crew down here in 1964 to document it. But back in the days when CBS was one of only three channels available to American viewers, the 45-minute documentary never aired publicly, Griffin said.

Perhaps, he surmised, in that era the white leaders could have suffered a public backlash merely for displaying goodwill and reason, possibly imploding the forward progress achieved. However, Griffin's DVD copy of "Quiet Conflict" shows that the documentary at least survives for posterity.

The film crew captured Brunswick in the throes of an awkward metamorphosis, transitioning from an archaic society to a community at least trying to live up to the American ideal that all are created equal. It captures more hope than hostility.

"He was a good man," Griffin says, as former Mayor Joe Mercer is interviewed.

Brunswick's City Manager at the time is quoted: "Our people, very wisely, we think, chose the bargaining table and resolved our differences."

By the mid-1960s, beaches, restaurants, hotels and many more public facilities had been desegregated. While it all came about without physical altercation, it was not without struggle, Griffin said.

Applying the pressure for change was the Rev. Julius Cesar Hope, pastor, local NAACP President and mentor to a fresh-out-of-college Griffin. "I was his lieutenant," Griffin said, as the determined lean face of the Rev. Hope fills the TV screen.

In one of many scenes focusing on him, the Rev. Hope describes favorable results achieved from picketing a white-owned grocery store that served mostly blacks but would hire none.

"We haven't picketed that store again," Hope says. "We haven't had to. We've had good cooperation."

The Rev. Hope goes on to discuss attempts to integrate a golf course on Jekyll Island and other inclusionary efforts.

"They didn't just give them to us," Rev. Hope says. "The better thinking people in the town want to continue in the right direction ... for peace and harmony."

When the slow trickle of public school desegregation finally reached full fruition here in 1970, Griffin left Risley to teach at Brunswick High. (Griffin would see his five children grow up in the county school system.) There he switched from music teacher to guidance counselor. You see, Griffin did not help bust the barrier in order to simply stand around enjoying the view on other side.

Having secured access to greater opportunity, Griffin busied himself in public service to all. And with two masters degrees and a doctorate of law degree, he had much to give. In addition to his education career, Griffin served as a county tax assessor, a zoning commissioner, a federal selective service board member and a hospital authority board member.

"That's what it was all about," Griffin says. "It felt really good to be a part of that change."

Old Sidney Lanier Bridge marked by tragedy, endurance

Something went wrong that night aboard the African Neptune, which was 13 minutes out of the Port of Brunswick with a full load of naval stores.

The 16-year-old Sidney Lanier Bridge's center draw spans dutifully opened for passage through the Brunswick River. But it became increasingly clear to those waiting in vehicles on the bridge that the U.S. freighter was off course. Also, it was not stopping.

Crew members would later attribute the ship's wayward trek to a "steering failure," according to an *Associated Press* report. They dropped anchor in an effort to stop its trajectory toward the Sidney Lanier Bridge, but the anchor apparently could find no purchase in the riverbed below.

It kept on coming.

"Someone screamed that the ship was going to hit the bridge," Glynn Police Chief A.L. Lockey told *The New York Times*. "So they got out of their cars and started running off the bridge."

Not all of them, not enough of them. "Others, he said, sat frozen in their vehicles," *The Times* reported, illustrating the national buzz the crash became.

And so then 11,000 tons of floating steel slammed into the Sidney Lanier Bridge, on top of which many found themselves trapped. The disaster occurred in the waning hours of Nov. 7, 1972, on a Tuesday night described by a bridge maintenance engineer as "pitch black," according to the AP.

The African Neptune crashed into the bridge about 350 feet south of the draw spans. The collision crumbled three 150-foot spans of the mile-long bridge. Worse still, 10 vehicles plunged into the swift currents of the 40-foot Brunswick River. Ten people died that night, among them four members of a Waycross family. Others who perished included a 19-year-old Brunswick woman, a Jacksonville man, a Savannah woman, a doctor from Kentucky and a 28-year-old man from Citrus, Fla., who was passing through on his honeymoon.

The big freighter "went plumb through" the bridge, bridge-tender Roscoe Tanner told the AP.

Eleven others were injured; many were rescued. Some survivors held to life preservers tossed into the water from the African Neptune. Tugboats and shrimp boats joined immediately in the search for survivors and bodies. The last five bodies were recovered on Nov. 11, according to *The Times*.

Among the survivors were Mary and Albert Donal, a Pennsylvania couple returning from a honeymoon in Florida. As they waited in line with other cars on the bridge for the ship to pass, then 36-year-old Albert Donal stepped out of the car and over to the rail to see what the holdup was.

"She said her husband got out of the car and went to the bridge rail to see what was wrong," the AP reported. "He was walking back when the 'bridge fell out from under us.'"

Both survived the disaster, reuniting at the local Brunswick Hospital emergency room.

Repairs to the damage took six months to complete, and cost $1.3 million. Interstate-95's construction through Glynn County had not been completed. The only detour option was via Ga. Highway 303 through Blythe Island.

In the final analysis, "steering failure" did not cause the deadly crash of the African Neptune. It resulted from a who's-on-first confusion of human errors on the bridge of the ship, according to the conclusions of the U.S. Coast Guard and the National Transportation Safety Board.

From a report released May 23, 1974:

"The National Transportation Safety Board determines that the probable cause of the collision of the SS African Neptune with the Sidney Lanier Bridge was (1) the failure of the helmsman to apply the correct rudder response to two helm orders; (2) the failure of the third mate, master, and pilot to discover the first error; and (3) the delay by the third mate, master, and pilot in detecting the second."

The majestic sweep of today's arching 480-foot-high Sidney Lanier Bridge has etched itself so iconically into our local skyline that it is sometimes hard to believe it was never there. But the cable-stayed bridge with a 185-foot clearance underneath has only been open since 2003. Its 1.5-mile-long stretch makes it the longest-spanning bridge in Georgia, longer even than its sister bridge in Savannah, the Talmadge Memorial.

The original Sidney Lanier Bridge was completed in June of 1956, connecting U.S. Highway 17 for the first time between the northern and southern banks of the Brunswick River. That horrific night in 1972 was not the only time the humble drawbridge of old gained national attention.

In fact, yet another ship struck the bridge in 1987. The Polish freighter Ziemba Bialostocka struck the draw span tower on May 3 of that year, causing $3 million in damage that took about five months to repair. Fortunately, there were no casualties that time.

All that remains today of the bridge is the section that juts out a couple of hundred feed into the north bank of the river beneath the present Sidney Lanier Bridge. It serves as a fishing pier and observation deck for Sidney Lanier Park.

But that old bridge can still be seen, usually late nights on channels that carry old movies. Fans of Burt Reynolds' movies have seen it often. The old Sidney Lanier Bridge is the setting for parts of the opening-scene chase in The Longest Yard.

That part where hero Paul Crewe (Reynolds) clears a rising drawbridge span, briefly losing the cops as Lynyrd Skynyrd's "Saturday Night Special" blares in the background? That's us, y'all.

Compared to the Spanish explorers, Oglethorpe was a historical newcomer

Long before British Gen. James Oglethorpe came to Coastal Georgia, there was Spain's Lucas Vázquez de Ayllón.

De Ayllón not only beat Oglethorpe to the Georgia Coast by more than 200 years, the settlement he established on our coastline is now recognized as the first European settlement in North America. (Excluding, of course, the temporary settlement in Newfoundland by the Viking Leif Erikson around 1000.)

The Spanish explorer established the mission settlement of San Miguel de Guadalupe in 1526, probably on the shores of Sapello Sound in McIntosh County. We are not sure exactly where it was, although archaeologists have been poking around for years trying find physical traces of its location. Our best evidence of the settlement comes from Spain's painstaking records-keeping practices.

The settlement included about 500 Spanish soldiers, settlers and Jesuit priests. Sadly, it also was the first venture to bring African slaves to the Americas. The settlement was short-lived, however, plagued by disease and starvation throughout. Hundreds perished here in a matter of months. The rest straggled back to Spain.

San Miguel de Guadalupe may be the continent's oldest European settlement, but it is a relative newcomer to documented American history. They were not teaching anything about it when

Artist's interpretation of Spanish mission San Miguel de Guadalupe.

popular Coastal Georgia historian and author Buddy Sullivan was a schoolboy back in Darien. The settlement was little known until noted historian and author Paul Hoffman, a professor at LSU, delved into 500-year-old Spanish records later on in the 20th Century to verify its existence.

De Avyllón's expedition set out with high ambitions and the King of Spain's edict for a lasting Spanish colony in the New World. No doubt contributing to the failure of the newcomers was their poor treatment and disdain for the native Guale natives, who might have been more willing to assist the struggling Spaniards otherwise. Among those who perished here was de Ayllón (1475-1526) himself.

Some still argue the settlement was actually established near the Pee Dee River in South Carolina, but a careful examination of evidence leans most historians toward a more likely location around the Sapelo Sound. Sullivan believes those archaeologists will eventually discover evidence of the colony locally, if through nothing else than the graves of the many who died here.

"Nobody's found anything yet," Sullivan has said. "I suspect one day somebody will."

The Spanish would return to Georgia's coast about 50 years later, establishing Franciscan mission settlements on St. Catharines, St. Simons and Cumberland islands. Santo Domingo was first established on the mainland near Darien, but later relocated to St. Simons Island's north end. There it was renamed Asajo.

The priests hoped to convert the native tribes, which consisted of Guale and Mocama. These natives had lived along the Georgia coast for some 6,000 years, growing familiar vegetables such as cantaloupe, squash and corn in the fertile spongy soil and reaping the bounty of seafood and game that thrived here.

The missionaries' successes in converting the natives varied, wavering from mildly enthusiastic cooperation and compliance to indifference, mistrust and outright hostility. The latter emotion reached a boiling point in 1597 with a violent uprising led by the warrior Jaunillo, the disaffected son of a local Guale chieftain. The bloodshed left five priests dead, including Father Verascola at Asajo on St. Simons Island.

The Roman Catholic Diocese of Savannah has submitted the five slain priests with the Vatican for sainthood. A relief sculpture of the five "Georgia Martyrs" hangs in the lobby of St. William Catholic Church on St. Simons Island. Two of the other slain priests were killed on St. Catherine's Island at Santa Catalina.

This settlement's exact location remained undiscovered until archaeologist David Thomas Hearst uncovered it during an expedition on the island in 1982. The Diocese of Savanah consecrated the ground in honor of the priests in 1985.

Archaeologists have since gleaned a trove of Spanish and native artifacts from that site on St. Catharine's Island, including pewter ware, ceramics and religious medallions. Some of the items are on display at Fernbank Museum of Natural History in Atlanta.

The location of Santa Catalina, however, remains a closely guarded secret, known only to a handful of archaeologists, historians and other academic types. "Why do they keep it a secret?" Sullivan said. "Artifact hunters. Looters."

Spanish missions remained in operation up and down the Georgia coast through the 17th century, eventually giving way to pressure brought to bear by rival England's growing designs on expansion in the New World. But by the time Oglethorpe established Fort Frederica on St. Simons Island in the new British colony of Georgia in 1736, there was nothing new about Old World visitors to these shores.

Horton House still stands as a link to Jekyll's early settlement

For proof that they don't build 'em like they used to, stop in sometime at Maj. Horton's place up on the north end of Jekyll Island.

Ok, so it lacks windows and doors — no roof, either — and it looks like it hasn't been painted in centuries.

But never mind that. After all, the two-story Horton homestead has stood steadfastly for 275 years — the first-ever English settlement on Jekyll Island. Constructed of the locally-venerated concoction of oyster shells, lime and sand known as tabby, the sturdy Horton House has endured the Revolutionary War, the War of 1812, the Civil War and untold hurricanes and tropical storms.

Stop in and see for yourself sometime. The Horton House Historic Site is open to the public, located alongside Riverside Drive. It is maintained by the Jekyll Island Authority.

Its namesake, unfortunately, was not quite so durable. Maj. William Horton died in Savannah in 1749, just 13 years after arriving in Colonial Georgia. But Horton would prove essential in establishing the colonial foothold that would become the permanent settlement we know today as the Golden Isles. And the plantation manor he built on Jekyll Island would be called home by a succession of prominent founding families after Horton's demise.

The former Undersheriff of Herefordshire, England, arrived in Savannah in February of 1736, among a boatload of adventure-seeking soldiers recruited from England to protect the young colony of Georgia (est. 1732). Colony founder Gen. James Oglethorpe was keen to draw a defensive line in the sand between the British colony and their Spanish rivals to the south in Florida. Horton quickly gained access to Oglethorpe's confidence.

That same year, Oglethorpe placed Horton over a few dozen soldiers who arrived on St. Simons Island to build the foundation of Fort Frederica and its surrounding township. With a promotion to major, Horton was placed in command of the troops there.

For a job well done, the Colony's trustees granted Horton 500 acres on neighboring Jekyll. (The island, by the way, is named for English barrister and politician Sir Joseph Jekyll, a stalwart early backer of the Georgia colony.) Some defensive breastworks were built on Jekyll, but the island's main function was agricultural.

Horton was living on Jekyll by 1737. The original Horton House was constructed of wood. Around it, Horton raised cattle and grew the crops that fed the fort on the island next door. Additionally, he grew the hops and barely to brew the beer that slaked their thirst from toiling away all day in woolen clothing under the hot south Georgia sun.

With the nation's current craft beer craze taking firm root here in Georgia, it is a wonder no one has created a local lager or ale named for Horton. He established what is generally considered Georgia's first brewery. Oglethorpe originally banned hard liquor from the colony — beer and wine only.

The crops at Horton's estate were tilled by indentured servants, as colonial Georgia initially banned slavery. His estate included a barn, servants' quarters and a warehouse for storing beer, wine and other stocks for Fort Frederica.

The Battle of Bloody Marsh in July of 1742 on St. Simons Island proved to be a decisive victory for the British colonial interests in the Americas, but it was rotten luck for Horton. Still smarting from their drubbing on St. Simons Island, the retreating Spanish took out their frustrations on the two-story Horton House, burning it to the ground. The place was defenseless. On July 7, the day of the battle, Horton had mustered the smattering of troops he had on Jekyll and crossed the St. Simons Sound in broad daylight to join Oglethorpe in the defense of Fort Frederica, according to June Hall McCash, author of the book "Jekyll Island Cottage Colony."

Undeterred, in 1743 Horton rebuilt from the ashes, this time in tabby. The home had chimneys on either end; the first floor was divided into two rooms by a tabby wall and there were sleeping quarters on the second floor. Like all farming enterprises, the Horton estate experienced its ups and downs over the years, leading Horton to bemoan shortly before his death that "the labour was in vain" and it "was unfit for cultivation," according to McCash.

Chris Joiner, Jekyll Island Museum manager, and Cheltsey Vann, a program educator at the museum, stand outside Horton House. (Staff Photo/The Brunswick News)

But the estate was a pastoral postcard when a Mr. John Pye visited in August of 1746. Pye reports that Horton "has a very Large Barnfull of Barley not inferior to ye Barley in England, and about 20 Ton of Hay in one stack, a Spacious House & Fine Garden, a plow was going with Eight Horses."

After Horton's death in 1749, the spread became the estate of Capt. Raymond Demere, another key figure in the founding and defense of Fort Frederica.

Wealthy Caribbean landowner Clement Martin oversaw the land after Demere, although he likely never lived there permanently. The aristocratic French sea captain Christophe Poulain DuBignon established a plantation there in the 1790s, taking up residence in Horton's home and growing Sea Island cotton.

British troops ransacked the estate during the War of 1812.

But the plantation would remain in the DuBignon family up until the Civil War. After the war, John Eugene DuBignon and a brother-in-law bought up the whole of Jekyll Island and successfully pitched it to wealthy northern businessmen as a private hunting club. Their creation would become known as the Jekyll Island Club, the winter retreat of industrial magnates and power brokers who ruled over America's Gilded Age.

Throughout it all, the Horton House has stood tall.

Fort King George's "invalid regiment" laid groundwork for future city of Darien

By the early 18th century, the space between Charles Town in the British Colony of South Carolina and St. Augustine in Spanish Florida appeared to be as a good a place as any to pick a fight.

Spain claimed ownership of the land but had long since abandoned any efforts at settlement on what is now the Georgia coast. The British colonies to the north were by then on solid footing, and the empire was looking to stretch its legs farther south.

You might say Fort King George was established right in the middle of this no man's land in 1722 as a British dare to Spanish claims on the territory. The Spanish squawked a bit, but never took the bait presented by this British outpost in present-day Darien.

The only fight His Majesty's Independent Regiment of Foot saw was against disease. Scurvy, dysentery and malaria routed the regiment in its short-lived stay at the fort, which burned down five years later in 1727. These soldiers at Fort King George were more accurately his majesty's castoffs, a muster of old soldiers and those rotating off of sick call.

"They were known as the invalid regiment," said Valerie Ikhwan, Manager of Fort King George State Historic Site. "It definitely represented a kind of sad and challenging part of early Colonial history."

But it was an important part of our early history no less. That is why the state rebuilt an exact replica of Fort King George on the bluff at the mouth of the Altamaha River where the original structure once stood. The state historic site includes a 40-foot-high wooden blockhouse and barracks surrounded by a protective palisade gate, as well as an exterior

Fort King George State Historic Park.

moat, ramparts and picket breastworks. One authentic remnant is a cemetery containing the graves of 17 soldiers who succumbed to disease at the fort.

Artifacts from Fort King George's era include a swivel-gun cannon that actually guarded the original ramparts. A "great little video" plays regularly at the museum, explaining how such artifacts were used as well as how folks lived in the era, Ikhwan said.

"It was definitely a challenging outpost," she said.

Whatever the fort's shortcomings and failures, it laid the foundation for achieving its intended purpose. Gen. James Oglethorpe would later establish the Colony of Georgia in 1732. Originally known as New Inverness, Darien was incorporated as part of the new British Colony in 1736, making it the second oldest city in Georgia behind Savannah. That same year, Oglethorpe established Fort Frederica on St. Simons Island.

Built in part upon Fort King George's blueprint, Fort Frederica succeeded in goading the Spanish into a fight. At the Battle of Bloody Marsh in July of 1742 on St. Simons Island, the Spanish famously tucked tail and sailed for Florida, never to campaign north again.

Actually, the Spanish were the first Europeans to settle at the site of Fort King George, a natural choice given the Altamaha's use as an inland trade route and the bountiful supply of natural resources. The Guale indians had a village there when Franciscan Friars established Mission Santo Domingo de Taleje among them in 1595. Ill will among the natives they sought to convert led to violence, forcing the missionaries to relocate to the north end of St. Simons Island in 1661. Renamed Mission Santo Domingo Asao, this final Spanish footprint along Coastal Georgia was gone by the 1680s.

On behalf of the Colony of South Carolina, Col. John "Tuscarora Jack" Barnwell convinced British Parliament in 1720 that the mouth of the Altamaha River was a prime spot for staking expansionist claims in North America. A group of scouts under Barnwell set themselves to building Fort King George in 1721. It was completed a year later, centered on a three-story cypress log blockhouse — powder, ammunitions and supplies on the first level; gun and cannon emplacements on the second; lookout posts on the third.

Col. Barnwell earned his feisty nickname in clashes with the Tuscarora natives of the Carolinas. He expected troops worthy of his formidable reputation to man Fort King George. What he got instead were soldiers past their prime, mixed with invalids from the Royal Hospital in Chelsea, England.

Many did not survive the overseas trip. The fort was woefully undersupplied and ripe for disease from the start. Some 140 officers and men perished at the fort before fire destroyed it in 1727. The survivors limped back to military outposts in the Carolinas.

A decade later, however, a crack troop of Scottish Highlanders versed in guerrilla tactics, under the command of Oglethorpe, guarded a young timber community that we know today as Darien. The workers there incorporated cutting-edge technology for its day with the local natural resources, powering the saw mills by manipulation of those ever-dependable Low County tides.

"Darien quickly became a leader in timber production among the Colonies," Ikhwan said. "The mills were tidal-powered; they figured out how to use the tides to their advantage. And it all started with the establishment of Fort King George."

Fort King George Historic Site is open 9 a.m. to 5 p.m. daily, except Monday, and is located at 302 McIntosh Road. Admission is $7 for adults, $6.50 for seniors and $4 for youngsters. Call 912-437-4770 for information.

Hofwyl-Broadfield: Rice plantation endures as living history dating to Antebellum era

It is a state historic site these days, located off of U.S. Highway 17 in northern Glynn County.

But Hofwyl-Broadfield Plantation's living history as a working agricultural enterprise harkens to the era when Elton John's Crocodile Rock was a big hit and Clint Eastwood's High Plains Drifter was a top box office draw.

No kidding. The year was 1973, and estate matriarch Ophelia K. Dent had just sat down to morning coffee in the stately home's parlor on Sept. 5. A butler returning moments later found the 85-year-old had passed away quietly, sitting at a mahogany heirloom desk. Thus ended the 167-year run of a plantation estate that remained in operation under the same family, dating back five generations to estate founder William Brailsford in 1806.

It was simply a dairy farm at the end. And granted, nobody visits a historic plantation to relive the glory days of mood rings and pet rocks. But site manager Bill Giles said the plantation's longevity is significant. A tour of Hofwyl-Broadfield Plantation will take visitors on an authentic journey all the way back to Coastal Georgia's Antebellum period. But that story's narrative will remain from start to finish in the resilient hands of the Brailsford-Troup-Dent family.

"After the Civil War, industrialists from up north started buying up plantations for hunting lodges," Giles said. "But that never happened here. The family held out."

You will not find another Antebellum-era coastal plantation so well preserved along the coast between Jacksonville and Charleston, Giles said. And for good reason. The Hofwyl-Broadfield land was simply too valuable as an agricultural entity to sell out to Yankee hunters.

Giles stood above a high bluff on the home's front lawn Thursday morning, pointing a hand north across several hundred yards

133

Hofwyl-Broadfield Plantation home.

of pristine marsh stretching to a distinct, raised tree line. In the plantation's heyday of the 1850s, this marshland was all planted in rice fields. Those yonder trees sprout from the remains of a plantation dike. This land once comprised portions of the most expensive real estate in all of Georgia, Giles s aid.

Cotton might have been king elsewhere in the South, but rice reigned in the coastal Low Country. The region's extensive marsh system, freshwater estuaries and swift, dependable tides made it conducive to rice cultivation. By the 1850s, the region -- extending to coastal South Carolina -- led the world's commercial rice market.

And this prime spot in a broad bend of the Altamaha River was arguably the most prized rice real estate around, Giles said. The English-born Brailsford was a Charleston merchant who bought the "Broadface" property in 1806, renaming it Broadfield after establishing his rice plantation there.

Rice cultivation of the era was an elaborate process, involving complex details. The marsh was sectioned off into numerous low-lying fields bordered by high dikes. The land was irrigated by a system of floodgates, which would be opened with outgoing freshwater high tides.

Rice cultivation required intensive labor. Behind the pastoral veneer of Antebellum gentility, there is the heinous fact of slavery. At its pinnacle of production, this plantation held 357 enslaved persons, Giles said.

Plantations generally maintained two rice crops concurrently — an early crop planted in March and harvested in August, followed by a late crop from June to October. Several times a year the floodgates dictated irrigation and drainage for maintenance and harvest. The museum at Hofwyl-Broadfield features a detailed model of the rice fields, as well as replicas of the wooden floodgates.

Management of the plantation passed from Brailsford to his son-in-law, Dr. James M. Troup, the brother of Gov. George Troup. By the time Troup died in 1849, the plantation included 7,300 acres, stretching from the winding Atlamaha River all way to the present-day Marshes of MacKay neighborhood, Giles said.

Dr. Troup's daughter Ophelia Troup would marry George Dent. They built the historic site's existing home, named Hofwyl after the Swiss boarding school Dent attended.

The family fled during the Civil War years (1861-65), as did most white landowners hereabouts. They returned afterward, however, to keep the family rice concern going in the Reconstruction era, employing freedmen to work the land for wages. In fact, the plantation, much of it sold to pay taxes after the war, continued growing rice under this arrangement well into the 20th century. Hofwyl produced its last crop in 1917.

Dairying had long been a component of rice plantations, as the cows found good grazing among the stubble of harvested rice fields. Hofwyl continued operating as a dairy farm following its last rice harvest. And it was still a dairy farm on Sept. 5, 1973, when Ophelia Dent, granddaughter of George and Ophelia, sat down to coffee in the Hofwyl house. This Ophelia never married or had children and had long planned to leave Hofwyl-Broadfield to posterity.

She kept her promise to us. It is all there, pretty much as the Brailsford-Troup-Dent family left it. Even that chair and desk where Ophelia Dent breathed her last breath. "The plantation is fully furnished with antiques dating back to the late 1700s that have been in the family for generations," Giles said.

Hofwyl-Broadfield State Historic Site is open 9 a.m. to 5 p.m., Wednesday through Sunday. Call 912-264-7333 for information.

Hofwyl-Broadfield's little kepi has big story

I nside his office at the museum at Hofwyl-Broadfield State Historic Site, Bill Giles slips on a pair of white gloves. He tenderly picks up a little red cap, handling it gently, with care and respect.

It is a Confederate kepi, or military cap. The red indicates it was worn by an artilleryman, explains Giles, the estate's Historic Site Manager. He notes the intricate gold braiding, which indicates its wearer carried the rank of captain.

The cap looks almost new, but this is no replica. It is the real deal. This kepi was actually worn more than 150 years ago by Confederate Capt. George C. Dent, then the patriarch at this plantation on a bend in the Altamaha River in northern Glynn County.

And there is yet another detail that pinpoints this cap to the Civil War era (1861-65). It really is a little cap. This thing could scarcely cover the bald spot on a modern-day middle-aged American man. The average Rebel or Yankee soldier of the day stood 5 foot 7 and weighed about 140 pounds. Today's average American man is nearly 5 foot 10 and weighs about 195.

"You can see how tiny, how very small it is," Giles said, taking care not to touch the cap with his gloved index finger while pointing out the details. "People simply were not as big back then as they are now."

Capt. Dent's kepi is now on display in the family's plantation house at Hofwyl-Broadfield State Historic Site, 5556 U.S. Highway 17. It is in good company. Everything inside the 1850s two-story plantation home, from the late 18th century Cantonese china to the 19th century furniture, are possessions of the Brailsford-Troup-Dent family that called the estate home.

Faye Cowart, a historical interpreter at the site, rediscovered the captain's kepi about five years ago while sorting through some old boxes at the home. Time had taken its toll on this little historic artifact.

"When we first found it, it was kind of deteriorated," Giles said.

Giles had the cap sent to the state historic sites system's preservation lab in Atlanta, where it languished for lack of money. Then some distant kinsmen came to the rescue.

A local Sons of Confederate Veterans outfit contacted Giles one day to ask if there was anything the group could do to help out with historic preservation at Hofwyl-Broadfield. Giles did not have to think twice. The weathered kepi's cause was a perfect fit for the Confederate sons of Thomas Marsh Forman Camp 458's offer of assistance.

The group sold tickets at $10 a pop for the chance of owning a dazzling quilt created by Libby Carter, wife of member J.C. Carter. One lucky ticket holder got a beautiful quilt for $10 and Hofwyl-Broadfield received more than $800 for the kepi's restoration.

The local Sons of Confederate Veterans also raised money recently for the U.S. Military Veterans Lounge at the College of Coastal Georgia, said group Commander Hal Crowe.

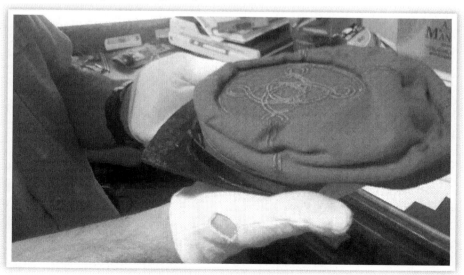

This kepi from the Civil War is on display at Hofwyl-Broadfield State Historic Site.

"We're trying to do more for the community," Crowe said.

The group's donated money to Hofwyl-Broadfield went to good use, as you can see for yourself now that the kepi is on display. The restoration was done by two separate specialists — one worked on the cloth and the other worked on the leather brim, Giles said.

Capt. Dent likely wore the kepi during one of two tours of duty: his early stint as captain of artillery on St. Simons Island and his time in the waning years as captain of artillery in Savannah, Giles said. Both posts were uneventful, as far as military action. The Confederates abandoned St. Simons Island to advancing Yankees in March 1862 after demolishing the lighthouse. Union Gen. William Tecumseh Sherman famously made a Christmas present of Savannah to President Lincoln in December 1864 without firing a shot inside the city limits.

However, Capt. Dent's wartime service was by no means uneventful or without risk. He suffered a wound to the arm during fighting at the Battle of Jackson, Miss., in May 1863. Dent also took part in the fighting at Chattanooga, Tenn., later in the war, Giles said.

Rebellion ran in the family. Dent was a second cousin to Confederate Gen. James Longstreet, one of Gen. Robert E. Lee's most trusted adjutants and military strategists.

Young James Dent was barely a teenager when the war began. But he joined the Confederate Army at 15, primarily serving as a color bearer and signal corpsman in North Carolina.

When the war ended with Lee's surrender at Appomattox Courthouse, the venerated general basically told his soldiers to go home and become good American citizens. The Brailsford-Troup-Dent family apparently took that advice to heart.

Although many plantations were gone with the wind at war's end, rice cultivation continued here until well into the early 20th Century. Former slaves, returning as freedmen, worked the fields for wages. After the rice-growing days waned early in the 20th century, the homestead survived as a dairy farm until 1973.

Like all the other attractions at Hofwyl-Broadfield, that little red kepi has big historic tale to tell.

Jekyll Island: From elite retreat to public treasure

Coastal Georgia's natural beauty is rarely more accessible to the public than on Jekyll Island. A stroll or bicycle ride through its wending nature trails can put you in touch with some of this area's most pristine coastal settings.

And while enjoying the flora and fauna that is so carefully preserved on parts of Jekyll Island, you can thank some of the most ruthless industrialists and power brokers in American history. No kidding. The island's present protected status can trace its inception to the Gilded Age of the late 19th century, when Jekyll was the private playground of Rockefellers, Morgans, Vanderbilts, Pulitzers and other turn-of-the-century titans.

Most everyone around here knows at least an inkling about the storied Jekyll Island Club. Remnants of that reign of the nation's wealthy elite (1886 - 1947) are readily evident still today. Folks can visit William Rockefeller's Indian Mound cottage or tour the Jekyll Island Historic District and see it for themselves.

But the sight of a bird of prey plucking lunch from a lazy creek winding through an unblemished marsh near Jekyll's Driftwood Beach also is a legacy of these avaricious tycoons. The conservation movement as we know it today was hardly the point of the Jekyll Island Club, which a popular national magazine of the era described as "the richest, the most exclusive, the most inaccessible club in the world."

But the truth is, these upper crust snowbirds really loved Jekyll Island just the way they found it. Except for the clubhouse, several extravagant cottages and a golf course, they barely touched the place. Coastal Georgia historian Buddy Sullivan considers the Jekyll Island Club's exclusive membership among the region's first conservationists.

The Jekyll Island Club in its heyday.

By the time the progeny of the club's founders had grown bored of Jekyll and migrated south to Palm Beach and Miami, exclusive ownership of the island had left it pretty much unblemished. The state of Georgia bought the island for $675,000 in 1947 and opened it to the public as a state park a year later.

Jekyll Island's journey from private ownership to public preservation is a pattern Sullivan traces all along the coast in his book, "The First Conservationists?: Northern Money and Low Country Georgia, 1866-1930." In the decades following the Civil War, rich Yankees bought up six of Coastal Georgia's eight barrier islands. This included Howard Coffin (Hudson Motors) on Sapelo Island, Thomas Carnegie (steel, brother of Andrew) on Cumberland Island and John Wanamaker (retail/marketing pioneer) on Ossabaw Island.

"This to me was the first real conservation movement in Coastal Georgia," Sullivan said recently. "They fell in love with the ecosystem and environment of our Georgia Coast. That is why I've called them the first conservationists."

But back to Jekyll Island. British Gen. James Oglethorpe built an outpost there in the 1730s, after establishing Fort Frederica next door on St. Simons Island. He named the island for Sir Joseph Jekyll, a barrister and politician who supported Oglethorpe in founding the Colony of Georgia.

Oglethorpe later granted Jekyll Island to Maj. William Horton, who established a plantation using indentured servants to grow food for the Frederica settlement. Horton died in 1749. The two-story remnants of his 18th century estate are open to the public at Horton House on Jekyll Island.

By the 1790s, the island wound up in the hands of Christophe Poulain DuBignon, an aristocratic French sea captain who made his mark and his fortune as a privateer. The Dubignon family's cotton plantation thrived for the next several generations, although British troops ransacked the place and liberated nearly 30 slaves during the War of 1812.

Emancipation of all slaves and the end of the Antebellum era came with the South's defeat in the Civil War. So John Eugene DuBignon and his brother-in-law Newton Finney, who served as an officer in the Confederate Army, turned to the only people with money to burn at the time: rich Northerners.

The great-grandson of the DuBignon patriarch, John Eugene DuBignon busied himself buying up the whole of Jekyll Island. Finney, the former Confederate, wooed New York financiers on the idea of a private hunting club on Jekyll Island. It must have been a big hit. The tight-knit group of movers and shakers bought Jekyll outright from the two shrewd Southern salesmen in 1886.

And thus, the Jekyll Island Club was born. From Christmas through Easter these barrier island barons would while away their days amid luxury and mild Southern breezes on their own private island.

And it remains there still for us to see, pretty much as they left it. Their Jekyll Island Club is now the heart of the Jekyll Island Club Resort, a registered Historic Hotel of America. In addition to Indian Mound, there is the Goodyear Cottage, the DuBignon house and J.P. Morgan's San Souci, considered the first condominium building.

That is not all. There is that sparkling shimmer on still waters as a blue heron stalks the marsh for his supper, the spartina grasses cast in shades of green and gold by the setting sun. I am most partial to that legacy.

Thanks, gentlemen.

Tom Floyd's journey: Tale of the Wanderer

I t was my privilege to have known Karen Ward for a short while before she died in July of 2016.

She had no reason to think well of me after our first meeting, in which I called her out of the blue on a Sunday night, desperate for information to complete an article promised to Golden Isles Magazine. She was gracious nevertheless, filling in the article's missing link regarding her family's connection to the notorious slave ship, Wanderer.

Afterward, Karen was always friendly and engaging when I encountered her around St. Simons Island, whether it be Islands Planning Commission meetings at the Casino, the parking lot outside Winn Dixie, or in the takeout line at Southern Soul. Tall and elegant, I could not help but think she carried herself with a regal bearing.

She got that from the slave Tom Floyd, Karen would have told me if I had asked.

The storyline connecting Tom Floyd and Karen Ward is one of ignominy and promise, one that encompasses both America's shortcomings and its dream fulfilled. It also includes a native son of St. Simons Island who would attain the pinnacle of recognition in his sport.

Tom's story began long before the Wander landed in 1858 on Jekyll Island with more than 400 slaves. And it is not over yet.

There was certainly no worse maritime enterprise than the slave trade, which hauled captured Africans to the Americas in a horrific Atlantic crossing that was as deadly as it was brutal. So reprehensible was the trans-Atlantic slave trade that it was banned in the U.S. in 1807 at the behest of President Thomas Jefferson, himself a Virginia slaver owner.

Slavery and the buying and selling of humans in bondage persisted in Southern states up until the Civil War (1861-65) settled the issue once and for all. Technological innovations like Eli Whitney's cotton gin, invented in 1793, only created a greater demand for slaves by making cotton production all the more profitable.

The Wanderer.

Enter smuggling ships such as the Wanderer. The 106-foot schooner was built on Long Island, N.Y., in 1857, originally intended for more pleasurable pursuits. But it was sleek and fast, just the ship needed by prospective slave smuggler William C. Corrie.

Corrie and the Wanderer arrived on the African coast somewhere near present-day Angola on Oct. 5, 1858. The ship set off about two weeks later with 489 captured human beings. Some 409 of these captives survived, landing with the Wanderer at Jekyll Island near sunset on Nov. 28, 1858. Jekyll was owned at the time by John and Henry DuBignon, believed to be co-conspirators in the smuggling operation.

The enterprise apparently was not too clandestine, as the ship's arrival created something of an uproar. Corrie and other defendants later were acquitted of slave smuggling, although the court cases drew attention from New York to Washington to London. Most of the captives were moved immediately out of the area to avoid detection, eventually being sold in slave markets in Savannah, Augusta and South Carolina.

One teenage boy, however, was sold to Capt. Henry Floyd of Camden County. His African name was Ndzinga (or Mazinga). His new name would be Tom. He was captured along the Congo, Karen

Ward told me. Some historical accounts show he was trained in carpentry by Capt. Floyd. Ward told me he also was a playmate for the captain's son, a role often assigned to some slaves.

At any rate, young Tom's bondage was short-lived. Lincoln's Emancipation Proclamation was issued in January of 1863, followed by the Civil War's end in April of 1865.

Capt. Floyd, as well as Tom, were living in Brunswick by then. Now a free man, Tom took the captain's surname and went on to buy a piece of land on St. Simons Island's south end. Tom Floyd built a home there. He gained a reputation in the community as a healer, using knowledge inherited from his African forebears about the medicinal properties of plants and roots. Tom married a woman named Charity; together they had three children: Nora, Lincoln and Caesar Prince. (Tom had four children from an 1860 marriage to an enslaved woman named Silva, who later moved north during Reconstruction.)

Tom's 1883 obituary in the Brunswick Advertiser and Appeal described him as a "noted African," though it was less respectful of his reputation as a "medicine man."

Karen explained to me that Tom very likely came from a royal line, as there was a Queen Ndzinga from the region of his capture. Tom's great-great-grandson has since acquired what passes for royal status in America. Jim Brown's punishing running style with the Cleveland Browns in the 1950s and '60s earned him entry in the Pro Football Hall of Fame. Many consider him the best NFL running back ever.

Ward was Brown's daughter. She was Tom Floyd's great-great-great-granddaughter. She was much more than that to the Golden Isles. Karen was a member of the St. Simons Island African American Heritage Coalition and a board member of the Friends of Harrington School. Additionally, Karen served on the Islands Planning Commission and Brunswick's Urban Redevelopment Agency. At the time of her death, Karen headed up the The Wanderer Project, hoping to bring more attention to the slave ship and its ties to Jekyll Island.

This community experienced a deficit with her passing, just as it is a much better place for being able to claim Tom Floyd as one of us.

State Holiday
still rebel memorial
for some

Robert A. Browne's violin somehow ended up entrusted to my care, reaching me after being transferred through a myriad of hands on Mamma's side of the family.

This distant relative of mine carried the violin "during the war years," according to an index card that a previous caretaker had attached to the musical relic. The card refers to the years of the Civil War. Browne served the Confederate States of America as a captain in a Mississippi cavalry regiment.

I have no idea what motivated Capt. Browne to fight for the Confederacy. Even casual research of the broad spectrum of his confederates reveals a multitude of reasons why they went to war, contrasting in complexity with the stated goals of the slave-holding nation for which they fought.

But we are blood kin, the Captain and I. And that violin is a tangible connection to one of the most important episodes in American history. Though unintentionally, I have been a fairly poor steward of Captain Browne's family legacy.

However, the memory of John Givens of the 24th Georgia Infantry Regiment has been much more fortunate. The local chapter of the Sons of Confederate Veterans has taken great care to honor his grave at Oak Grove Cemetery in Brunswick, as well as those of hundreds of his Confederate comrades who are buried there and at cemeteries throughout the Golden Isles.

In case you forgot, Monday (April 23, 2018) is State Holiday in Georgia. But the fourth Monday in April is still Confederate Memorial Day to men like J.C. Carter of the Thomas Marsh Forman Sons of Confederate Veterans. This paid state holiday once paired itself with the official Confederate Memorial Month, both of which roughly mark the anniversary of the South's sur-

Violin carried by Capt. Robert A. Browne. (Photo by Lee Kelly)

render to Union forces in April of 1865.

So why does Carter still continue to honor the Confederate dead, even after the state's new official line is one of bureaucratic ambiguity? He does so mainly for Joshua Thomas Denton. The private with the 50th Georgia's Company C never wanted to leave his Coffee County farm in the first place. And he never returned.

Just as I am uncertain of Capt. Browne's motives, Carter is not quite sure why his great great-great grandfather went off to war.

Joshua was born in Telfair County in 1835. He and brother John and sister Mary were raised on an uncle's plantation after they were orphaned by an unnamed epidemic. By the time the Civil War broke out in 1861, Joshua owned a 265-acre farm, where he and wife Barbara were raising three young daughters.

Joshua and his brother John owned one slave between them, a man named Smart. But Joshua tended the livestock and sowed the farm's corn crops with his own sweat and toil, Carter said.

There appears to have been a local recruitment campaign that may have prompted Joshua and his brother John to enlist in the 50th Georgia in May of 1862.

"I've never read why he joined," Carter said. "He owned his own farm and he did his own work on the farm. He didn't have any reason to go fight, other than just being from Georgia."

Carter is the keeper of a dozen letters Joshua wrote home from the war. All speak of his desire to be back there.

"In all his letters, the only thing he wants to do is get back home to his farm," Carter said. "In every letter, he wants to know how the farm is doing, how the sheep and cattle are doing, the children. He just wanted to be home."

The Denton brothers were in Fredericksburg, Va., by December of that year, but their regiment did not take part in the decisive Confederate victory there. Joshua still had not had his baptism of fire by the spring of 1864, when a major battle began brewing in nearby Chancellorsville, Va. On May 3, the Georgia 50th was called into action to stave off a rear assault by the Union.

In the Battle of Salem Church, Joshua's troops were running low on ammunition when they mounted a desperate bayonet charge to repel the Union advance. This resulted in a rebel rout, putting the Union troops to flight.

It is not clear whether Joshua was struck by a musket ball or stabbed by a bayonet that day in his first and only fighting. However, the wound only worsened. His brother cared for him all the while. Joshua died in John's arms on May 11.

John buried his brother near Salem Church. The location of Joshua's grave was lost to time and war.

But down at the corner of Martin Luther King Jr. Boulevard and Mansfield Street in Brunswick, a Confederate memorial flag flutters above the grave of Benjamin A. Fahm in Oak Grove Cemetery. Carter and others with the SCV made sure that Fahm's service with the 4th Georgia Cavalry is not forgotten.

This Saturday, Carter and other SCV members will dress in Confederate reenactment uniforms for a small parade down Newcastle Street to Hanover Square. There they will be joined by local Daughters of the Confederacy members for a genteel picnic. Brunswick's first African-American mayor, Cornell Harvey, has again been invited to attend this year's picnic.

"I was elected by everybody and I want to be there for everybody," Harvey said after reading a proclamation at the 2016 picnic. "And I'm a history buff, too."

So I ask Carter the inevitable 21st Century question about our shared 19th Century ancestors. Politely, patiently, he explains his interest is about history and heritage. Nothing else.

"There was not a thing right about slavery and I'll be the first to tell you that," Carter said. "Some kids played cowboys, but I played Civil War when I was a boy. I have just always been interested in the Civil War."

From slave to soldier to farmer, freedom rings in Major Magwood's inspired journey

The life and times of Major Magwood provide us with a unique glimpse into the journey out of bondage for African-Americans in the tumultuous 19th Century along the Georgia Coast.

Major was born into slavery in South Carolina on a plantation owned by George Dent, who would be linked in marriage to the Hofwyl-Broadfield Plantation here in Glynn County. But by 1863, Major was a Union soldier in the 128th U.S. Colored Troops — a free man fighting for freedom.

Major would settle in Glynn County after the Civil War, where he and wife Mary Ann raised a passel of kids. Records indicate they lived amicably among ex-Confederate white neighbors. He died in 1910 at age 78 and was buried at Freedman's Rest Cemetery, located on Petersville Road in northern Glynn County.

History's big picture so often overlooks the Major Magwoods of yesteryear, the simple folks who quietly toiled, persevered and loved in measures larger than life. I stumbled upon Mr. Magwood's story Thursday while searching for information about Brunswick's historic Dixville community on GlynnGen.com, Amy Lynn Hedrick's immensely informative local history website.

Magwood's journey from enslaved man to freedom fighter was not unique. Union troops occupied much of the Georgia Coast by 1862. This left many an enslaved man with a quicker escape route to Union lines; still others were simply left behind by retreating slave owners.

"What varied in Georgia was not the desire of black people for liberty but their physical opportunity to obtain it," wrote historian Clarence L. Mohr in his book, Before Sherman: Georgia Blacks and the Union War Effort, 1861-1864. And, like the

Major Magwood and many other formerly enslaved men enlisted in the Union Army.

soldiers serving in the Confederacy, these black soldiers were fighting for their homeland, Mohr asserted.

"Northern recruiters discovered early that the prospect of securing the freedom of friends and relatives was a powerful inducement for blacks to join Union ranks," he writes. "Or, taking the opposite viewpoint, blacks soon discovered that the Union army offered an effective vehicle for rescuing family members still held in bondage."

Many a Sapelo Islander invested his newfound freedom in a rifle and marching orders, according to GlynnGen.com. Family records preserved by islanders show newly-freed men such as Sam Robert, Mars Carter, Peter Maxwell and Quatner Johnson enlisting in the Union Army. Jim Walker enlisted under the name James Spalding, the surname likely a nod to island's plantation family.

Island-born Shederick Mungen remained enslaved as late as 1861, but was a free man by the time of his enlistment in the 33rd U.S.C.T.'s B Company in December of 1862 at Beaufort, S.C. Sadly, he died of "dropsy" in a hospital in September of 1864.

Major Magwood enlisted in the 128th's Company A in March of 1863 at Hilton Head, S.C., records show. Major held the rank of corporal in March of 1866 when he was honorably discharged at Morris Island, S.C.

His wife, Mary Ann, had been enslaved on Hofwyl-Broadfield, where she was born in 1843. Magwood and Mary Ann were married by a Rev. Nelson in Glynn County, but there is confusion over whether this occurred before or after the Civil War. However, some evidence suggests that Mary Ann and Major knew each other before freedom, and that he had spent time in Glynn County prior to the war. Major's birthdate was recorded in at least one plantation journal held here by the Hofwyl-Broadfield side of the family, according to GlynnGen.

He and Mary raised 13 kids in a community known as Evelyn, apparently near Hofwyl-Broadfield in northern Glynn County. He was a farmer. He received an $8 monthly veteran's pension, which was upped to $12 a month in the 1890s and then to $15 by 1908. By the 1890s, a hernia suffered while unloading coal barges on an Army detail in 1865 began to take its toll on Major.

Former Confederates assisted the black Union veteran in keeping up with his pension beginning in the early 1890s, according to GlynnGen. In 1894, Dr. Judson Butts attested to Major's rheumatism and a nagging injury from an old gunshot wound. In 1898, J.E. Lambright and L.B. Davis both vouched for his good character and asserted that Mr. Magwood came by his injuries in honest service to his country and "not from any vicious behaviors." All three men were Confederate veterans.

"It appears that even though he was a former slave and a Union soldier, his Confederate neighbors helped him file all the proper documents, even attesting to his character when needed," the GlynnGen article states.

Major was illiterate, but he did learn to sign his name in a jagged cursive to replace the "X" he used on his early pension filings. Perhaps Major's best epitaph is his humble, utilitarian introduction to a 1903 affidavit to the pension board.

"I can't tell my age. I reckon I am over 70. My P.O. Is Evelyn, Ga. I am a farmer. I am the Major Magwood who served as a corporal in Company A … during the war of the Rebellion."

Family tree grew strong within rural Needwood community

Needwood Baptist Church has stood resolutely on its grounds beside U.S. Highway 17 in northern Glynn County for some 140 years. It was built by former slaves, who quite clearly intended to stake a lasting claim to the promise of freedom.

They would later invest the harvest of that promise in the construction of a one-room schoolhouse, which has sat steadfastly beside the church for more than 100 years. Both were the foundation upon which a tight-knit African-American community once persevered, placing their faith in strong family bonds and resourceful self-reliance.

Those traditions and values were still at the heart of the thriving Needwood community when Alfreda Grant-White was growing up next door to the church in the 1960s. Her dad Alfred Grant kept milk cows, goats and chickens; the family grew their own vegetables.

Her cousin, Malcom Harris, learned to fish, hunt and trap animals from their mutual grandfather, William Polite. Raccoons were a favorite prey, recalls Harris, 52, who grew up attending Needwood Church in the 1970s.

Laura Polite-Grant, 79, has no use for raccoon meat these days, but she recalled off the top of her head the process of preparing these crafty critters for the dinner table. Laura attended first- through seventh-grade in the Needwood schoolhouse with about 15 other children back in the 1940s and '50s. Laura, who graduated from Risley High, is Alfreda's Mom and Malcom's aunt.

William Polite was Laura's dad. He was born in 1900 and lived until 2000. William most certainly learned reading, writing and arithmetic in that schoolhouse, which would have been new at the time. In addition to sharing his knowledge of how to live off the land, William passed on valuable life lessons to the youngsters who grew up in the Needwood community.

"When he spoke, you would think you were listening to the Book of Proverbs," Alfreda said. "He was full of words of wisdom on how to live your life and how to conduct yourself."

William worked also at Broadfield Plantation, which held strong family ties for the Polites. He worked as a grounds-keeper and maintenance man at the dairy farm up until 1973, when Ophelia K. Dent died, and the plantation became a state historic site. (Prior to that, it had remained in agricultural operation under the Dent-Hofwyl-Broadfield family for more than 160 years.)

William followed in the footsteps of his father, Morris Polite, who was born in 1870 and also worked at Broadfield. Morris grew up around the time the initial phase of Needwood Church was raised. The congregation first established itself on Broadfield in 1866 as Broadfield Baptist Church. Needwood Baptist Church was built sometime during the 1870s. Morris might have been among the craftsmen who installed the twin towers at the church entrance in 1885.

Morris's father was a man named London, who was born into slavery on the Broadfield Plantation. As a freedman, he returned to the area to work for the Dent family at Broadfield. And he very likely took part in the initial construction of Needwood Baptist Church.

It is likely impossible for us to fathom how proud London would be of his great-great grandchildren, Alfreda and Malcom. Both children grew up in that country Needwood hamlet, attending services in the church their ancestors built.

The cousins went in to town to attend public school, Alfreda graduating from Brunswick High and Malcom graduating from Glynn Academy. Alfreda earned an academic scholarship to attend Albany State University. She went on to pursue a fulfilling teaching career in Savannah, where she lives today in retirement.

Malcom works as an assistant pathologist at the Glynn County Medical Examiner's Office and as assistant director at Brunswick

Alfreda Grant-White, Laura Polite-Short and Malcolm Harris all grew up within the rural community centered around Needwood Baptist Church. (Photo by Bobby Haven.)

Funeral Home. He is an avid fisherman and lives just down the road from Needwood Church.

But folks no longer gather to worship in the church and have not for several years. Most of the community's older folks have passed on, and the younger ones have all moved away. The community can no longer sustain a congregation.

The school, long ago relegated by progress to a community

hall for the church, now serves as little more than a storeroom for pews and chairs and books and such. The whitewash exterior of both buildings is faded and flaking, exposing the weathered old wood beneath to the elements.

Needwood Church and School are listed on the National Registry of Historic Places, but time does not care about that. Time is relentless, patient, unyielding.

However, Sonny Seals of the Atlanta-based nonprofit Rural Historic Churches of Georgia, has intervened on behalf of this important piece of local history. In the spring of 2018, his group submitted Needwood Church and School for consideration as one of the National Trust for Historic Preservation's 11 Most Endangered Places in America. The designation would bring nationwide attention to the little church's plight, giving it a better chance of raising the money needed for restoration and preservation.

Folks like Laura and Alfreda and Malcom would like that very much.

"When I look back now, I had a really good childhood," Alfreda said. "Survival was the main thing they concentrated on — and they did that by keeping the family together and worshiping together and sharing the love and all the blessings and the harvest from the field. I am forever grateful that I was able to take part in that."

Modest vessel Kit Jones left big wake in history of Sapelo Island, Coastal Georgia

When tobacco heir R.J. Reynolds took Sapelo Island off the hands of his friend Howard E. Coffin back in 1934, the Hudson Motor Co. founder threw in his luxury yacht Zapata at a sweetheart of a deal, $50,000.

The 124-foot Zapata was a prominent feature of the high-end style of entertaining Coffin became known for on Sapelo Island, where he restored Thomas Spalding's Sapelo House mansion to its pre-Civil War glory and played host to the rich and famous of the early 20th century. But the ritzy Zapata fairly paled in comparison to Reynolds' more modest Sapelo Island boat.

For its usefulness, versatility and perseverance, the most renowned vessel from Reynolds' time on the island is hands down the Kit Jones — the little tugboat that could. Although classified as a tugboat, the 60-foot craft was more accurately a transporter of freight and folks. It supplied Reynolds' operations on Sapelo, while ferrying the island's mostly Geechee population to and from the mainland.

And the Kit Jones did its duty during World War II as well, recruited into the Coast Guard as a fireboat patrolling the Port of Savannah.

Then, beginning in the 1950s, the boat served marine biologist Eugene Odum's groundbreaking studies that took place on Sapelo Island to gain a better understanding of the complex ecological balance within Georgia's coastal marsh system.

And the Kit Jones just kept going. It continued serving as a marine biology research vessel at the University of Georgia's Skidaway Institute near Savannah into the 1980s. The University of Mississippi acquired the boat for research in the Gulf of Mexico in 1985. The Kit Jones rebounded after being capsized

Sapelo Island's workhorse utility tug, the Kit Jones.

during Hurricane Katrina and continued to assist Ole Miss's marine researchers until 2013.

Still, the Kit Jones has one more destiny to fulfill. Its final journey will be an overland road trip from the Gulf Coast back home to McIntosh County. That is the intention of its newest owners, the McIntosh Rod and Gun Club. The group believes the Kit Jones is worthy of salvation and plans to someday open it as a museum on the Darien waterfront.

Their designs have merit — so says the Georgia Trust for Historic Preservation, which in November of 2017 included the Kit Jones on the state's top 10 list of "Places in Peril." It is the first boat ever to make the cut in the 13 years the Georgia Trust has issued its list of imperiled places.

"The Kit Jones is a very compelling, very good story," said Mark McDonald, the trust's president and CEO. "It's a very human story."

Indeed. Through its exhaustive service on the Georgia Coast, the Kit Jones intertwined itself in much of the coast's odyssey through the 20th century. And for all its workmanlike reputation, the Kit Jones is of noble origins and bears a genteel namesake.

When Reynolds decided he needed a vessel to serve his island compound, he turned to Sparkman & Stephens, an esteemed New York City marine design outfit. The boat's construction took place on Sapelo Island between 1938-39, under the direction of Danish-born shipbuilder Alex Holger Sparre of Brunswick. Its wood hull was comprised of heart-of-pine framed around a live oak rib-cage, all of the trees timbered on Sapelo Island.

Many of those taking part in its construction were islanders, the Geechee descendants of former enslaved people who had once worked Spalding's plantation. Many of those same residents crewed and piloted the Kit Jones in its active years on Sapelo during the 1940s. It was named for Katharine Jones, the wife of Alfred W. Bill Jones. Jones was a cousin and protege to Howard Coffin; together the two developed neighboring Sea Island into one of the premier resort destinations of its time.

Coffin sold his Sapelo Island holdings to Reynolds in the first place to keep Sea Island afloat after the 1929 Stock Market Crash. The $700,000 Reynolds paid for it did the trick; the resort island remained in the hands of the Jones family until the Great Recession of 2008.

Meanwhile, back on Sapelo, the Kit Jones was touching more lives than the swanky yacht Zapata ever could. It kept a steady flow of fuel and supplies moving onto this island that has never been bridged. Milk from Reynolds' dairy farm and other crops grown on the island made it to the mainland aboard her. From ferrying school children daily to taking expectant mothers on midnight runs to a needed doctor, the Kit Jones served the island's 500 residents in myriad ways.

While Reynolds was serving with distinction as a Naval commander in the Pacific during World War II, the Kit Jones was called up for coastal fireboat service from 1942-46. Reynolds' post-war interest in marine research led to the formation of the Georgia Marine Research Institute on 6,000 acres of Sapelo's pristine marshland. Odum's keen observations there led to a better understanding of our intricately-designed ecosystem and the vital need to preserve it.

His work also launched the Kit Jones' decades-long stellar tenure as a marine research vessel. Realizing the boat could be lost to posterity far from home in Gulf waters, the Rod and Gun Club stepped in several years ago and purchased the vessel. Now the club is trying to return her to more familiar waters.

Those wishing to lend a hand can donate at www.gofundme.com/researchvessel-kitjones.

Deaconess Alexander:
Footprints of a saint

Her lifelong journey of service to others ended more than 70 years ago, but Anna Alexander left behind the footprints of a saint on the sandy soil of Glynn and McIntosh counties.

Quite literally. Anna's calling as a teacher and spiritual leader kept her on the move in the late 19th century, a life of unceasing service to her God and His people. From her mission church in rural western Glynn County to her teaching duties in Darien, Anna walked much of the way, rowing by boat when waterways made it practical or necessary. She walked also to Brunswick to keep regular appointments with her spiritual mentors at St. Athanasius Episcopal Church.

This life of unselfish devotion did not go unnoticed in her own time, and her legacy of sacrifice shines still brighter today. Known then as Deaconess Alexander, the daughter of former slaves is now recognized as a Saint of Georgia by the state's Episcopal Diocese. Recognized in 1998, her Feast Day in the Georgia Episcopal Church is Sept. 24.

Anna's achievements earned still broader recognition in January of 2018. America's Presiding Episcopal Bishop, the most Rev. Michael Curry, lauded this homegrown saint during an Episcopal retreat at Honey Creek in Camden County. It was fitting, perhaps, that the nation's first African-American Presiding Bishop was there to applaud the first black Deaconess.

High praise, indeed. But the humble deaconess herself most likely would be more pleased with a less distinguished testimony to her legacy. Folks still gather regularly to worship at Good Shepherd Episcopal Church, the very church she founded in 1894. In addition to bi-monthly services at the church at 780 Pennick Road, the property at Good Shepherd includes the schoolhouse built at her behest and its frugal second floor apartment that Anna called home.

Anna was born sometime after the Civil War, the last of James

Deaconess Alexander.

"Aleck" and Daphne Alexander's 11 children. Her year of birth is something of a moving target, but she was most likely born in either 1878 or 1881. Her parents were enslaved by St. Simons Island plantation owner Pierce Mease Butler. Aleck, a personal servant to Butler, learned to read and write despite the prohibition of literacy among slaves.

At the end of the Civil War, the newly-freed Alexanders moved to the black community of Pennick, where Aleck became a carpenter and community leader. Young Anna made the most of the limited educational opportunities available to blacks at the time.

She started teaching as a young woman, beginning at a public school in the Pennick community. Later, she taught alongside her sister Mary at a school in Darien that was established by St. Cyprian's Episcopal Church. By this time, Anna also had developed a connection with St. Athanasius Episcopal Church in Brunswick. In 1894, with encouragement from St. Athanasius's Rev. J.J. Perry, Anna founded the mission church in Pennick that would later become Good Shepherd. She presided over outdoor services in the beginning.

Still teaching, Anna walked and rowed 40 miles round trip between her school children in Darien during the week and her flock in Pennick on weekends. In 1897, Anna moved briefly to Lawrenceville, Va., where she both taught and attended the teachers college at St. Paul's Normal and Industrial School.

She returned home around 1901 to find that the mission at Pennick had stagnated in her absence. It flourished upon her return. Anna worked as a seamstress to support herself, and more. In 1902 she bought the property on which her brother Charles would oversee construction of the first church. A school also was built on the site.

In the one-room schoolhouse, Anna taught children to read using the Episcopal Book of Common Prayer and the Bible. This African-American woman's exhausting commitment to the church did not go unnoticed by the white clergy of the time.

In 1907, Episcopal Bishop Cleland Kinloch Nelson consecrated her as a deaconess, a designation for women ordained and directed to serve God through caring for "the sick, the afflicted and the poor." Nelson praised Deaconess Alexander as a "devout, godly and respected colored woman."

That same year, however, a new Bishop of the Georgia Diocese snubbed African-Americans, silencing their voice in church matters and virtually cutting black churches off from state financial support.

If the church itself stopped giving, Deaconess Alexander and her Pennick church did not. Donating precious loose change, her congregation was consistently more giving toward charitable causes than any other in the diocese. In 1923, for example, the folks at Good Shepherd donated proportionately more money than all others to victims of a massive earthquake in Japan.

Also during this era, the existing church building at Good Shepherd was erected in 1928. Deaconess Alexander crusaded throughout the hard times of the Great Depression for government and private assistance to aid folks struggling in poverty, both black and white. In 1936, the very state bishop who had ostracized her and other blacks would laud the deaconess for her tireless service.

Deaconess Alexander died in 1947, ironically the same year the state diocese first invited blacks back to participate in the state convention. One wonders if the Deaconess and her congregation would have noticed. She spent a lifetime answering to a much higher authority.

Cutting edge 1900s technology, immigrants spurred local shrimping industry

A popular song by county music icon Willie Nelson famously heaps praise on cowboys as the epitome of the American free spirit.

It is a fine tribute. Personally, my heroes have always been shrimpers.

Having always lived in salty Southern air stirred by either Gulf or Atlantic breezes, I take comfort in the sight of those trawl nets flanking a shrimp boat as it rocks in the waves on a watery horizon. They are a stalwart breed, these hardy folks who defy the elements daily to wrest a living from the sea, harvesting perhaps the South's most prized seafood delicacy.

And the shrimp thriving in these local waters are particularly delicious, always have been. Some attribute the local stock's appetizing appeal to the Golden Isles' extensive saltwater marsh system, the most expansive on the Atlantic Seaboard. That marshland also serves as the nursery ground for our shrimp population.

There have been of lot of changes to the shrimping tradition around these parts, but the shrimp themselves have pretty much adhered to the same life cycle forever. There are two basic kinds of shrimp swimming in these waters: the larger white shrimp, which are caught mostly in the fall and winter months; and the smaller brown shrimp, which typically keep our shrimp boats chugging through the summer.

White shrimp swim offshore to spawn in the winter months, dying off after ensuring the fresh population of new shrimp. Those new larval shrimp grow to juveniles before heading inland to grow up in the nutrient-rich salt marsh waters, which are filtered and purified by those vast aquatic fields of spartina grasses. In the fall the adult shrimp head out to open waters again,

161

pursued relentlessly by those staunchly self-reliant saltwater cowboys, who insist that a bad day on the water shrimping is infinitely better than a good day on land working at the paper mill.

So familiar is the sight of shrimp boats plying our waters that a person might be led to think it has always been thus. Not so. While these tender crustaceans have long held appeal to our taste buds, shrimping as a viable local industry is barely 100 years old. Shrimping came into its own in the early 20th century, evolving into a thriving industry on the crest of emerging technology, improved fishing gear and an influx of proud immigrant stock with a seafaring heritage.

Before then, limited commercial fishing took place in the St. Simons Sound. It involved the grueling technique of furiously rowing 17-foot boats to encircle and trap shrimp within long nets. That is how Frank McDowell used to do it in the late 19th century off of Jekyll Island. McDowell was the great grandfather of Johnny Ray Bennett, a son of a son of a son of a shrimper who presently captains the 84-foot Flying Cloud out of the East River for the City Market seafood company in Brunswick.

Motorized boats were becoming more and more common in commercial fisheries by the early 1900s. Other rising technologies that boosted shrimping included refrigeration and ice machines, making it feasible to ship this Southern delicacy by railroad to parts north. Another advancement came from Boston transplant Billy Corkum, who settled in Fernandina Beach and modified an English-designed net to suit the needs of local shrimpers. The net was outfitted with weighted wooden doors, which opened the net's mouth wide under throttle as it was dragged along the bottom. This bit of ingenuity was the precursor to the otter trawl nets that are standard on shrimp boats today.

Brunswick's shrimping industry got another Old World boost after World War I, with the arrival of Portuguese immigrants who brought with them a long tradition of making a living from the sea.

The new arrivals' enthusiasm for harvesting Wild Georgia Shrimp and the nation's growing appetite for the same created a boom in Brunswick. It was not long before Brunswick was competing with Fernandina Beach and St. Augustine for the title of "Shrimp Capital of the World."

Capt. Johnny Ray Bennett's trawler, the Dora F.

Most of the Portuguese shrimpers have long since disappeared from the trade, but they brought with them one lasting tradition. The Blessing of the Fleet, which takes place in Brunswick each year on Mother's Day, is a joyful celebration held annually in shrimping villages from here to Bayou La Batre, near my hometown of Mobile, Ala.

The early years of shrimping proved profitable, giving rise to shipbuilding yards and seafood processing plants along the Brunswick and East rivers. First among them was the David Davis Co. in 1915. The company shipped processed boiled shrimp preserved in brine and packed in kegs to such distant destinations as Canada and England, according to the book *Brunswick: A Book of Memories.*

"Other shrimp were shipped in iced wooden boxes and sent to New York, or to specific customers in the Southeast," David Co. employee Richard Krauss reminisced in that book of memories.

That proud local shrimping tradition thrives still today, with tough-minded free spirits like Capt. Johnny Ray Bennett at the helm. Yeah, Capt. Johnny is a hero of mine.

If you have not done so already, please check out Larry's little book with the big title: *A Historical Crash Course on Coastal Georgia and the Golden Isles.* His first book on local history offers a quick, fun read full of intriguing facts and anecdotes on more than 500 years of local history here in this fascinating stretch of Coastal Georgia. It is based on local historian Buddy Sullivan's popular six-week lecture series at the St. Simons Lighthouse Museum. The book is available on Amazon and at several local book stores, gift shops, markets and museums on St. Simons Island and throughout the Golden Isles.

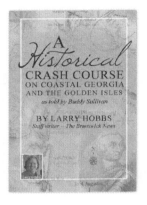

Made in the USA
Middletown, DE
31 July 2021